The Desert Shall Blossom

A Comprehensive Guide to Vegetable Gardening in the Mountain West

The Desert Shall Blossom

A Comprehensive Guide to Vegetable Gardening in the Mountain West

David E. Whiting

First Printing, May 1991

International Standard Book Number
0-88290-418-3

Horizon Publishers' Catalog and Order Number
1239

Printed and distributed
in the United States of America by

 Horizon
Publishers
& Distributors, Incorporated
P.O. Box 490 Bountiful, Utah 84011-0490

www.horizonpublishers.biz

Contents

1
Why Grow a Garden?

Gardening is America's number one leisure activity. It is a hobby for all Americans. Why do we spend our mornings, evenings and weekends vigorously digging in the soil, getting our hands dirty, and pulling weeds? There are several reasons.

The most common response to the question, "Why grow a garden," is "for the food." A U.S.D.A. study with the Expanded Foods and Nutrition Program found that a family which grows a garden typically has the recommended servings of fruits and vegetables in its daily diet. In contrast, families which do not grow a garden are very unlikely to have the recommended four servings of fruits and vegetables each day. Growing a garden has a major impact on a family's diet and health.

Home-grown vegetables can be eaten garden fresh, when their vitamin content is at its peak. Gardeners have control over additives, preservatives and the use of pesticides on their produce.

Growing a garden can save the family money. Considering the cost of seeds, fertilizer and water, a garden returns about ten fold on the investment.

A garden is a great place to teach children how to work. In modern society, children spend a lot of time being entertained by the TV or video games. Their opportunities to learn working skills are limited. Gardening is a great place for children to learn the rewards of labor. They can feel the pride of completing a challenging task even though it may not have been exciting and entertaining. They will learn that rewards for efforts are not always immediate. Gardening can be a great learning tool for family members to discover the joy and satisfaction found in work.

Gardening can also strengthen the family unit. A family which gardens, works, and plays together stays together. A generation or two ago, the typical family worked together on the family farm or in the family business. In most families today Dad, Mom and the kids each go separate ways during the day. A garden provides an excellent reason for the family to spend time together, working for a common goal. Sharp parents have their family members garden together as a group. They don't send the kids out to weed by themselves so it becomes a punishment. They go as a family, so gardening becomes a fun activity, instead of a chore. This gives Mom and Dad the opportunity to teach gardening skills to the children and opens the doors of communication about other important life topics.

Gardening is a great way to teach faith in God, the creator. It is an exercise in faith to plant seeds, with the hope of a bounteous harvest. It takes careful nurturing, weeding and tending for the seedling to mature into a useful plant. And tending the plants is truly an exercise in faith and hope—requiring faith that the plants will grow and hope that the yield will be abundant.

Another major benefit of gardening is for the gardener's mental health. Gardening is an excellent way to relieve stress. National studies repeatedly report that those with high stress jobs are more likely to garden. A good friend put it like this, "When I find myself upset about work, or frustrated with my wife and kids, I involve myself in working in my garden and my anger and frustrations melt away. I am refreshed. I have new prospective and my problems don't seem so serious any more." He takes his frustrations out on the weeds, not his family! A garden is a great place to bury anger, fears and worries. With a little care, they disappear, and corn, beans and tomatoes grow up in their place.

Yes, gardening truly is America's leading leisure activity for strong families and happy citizens!

2
Soil Management

The soil plays a major role in the growth of any plant. It serves to physically support the plant and offers the plant water and nutrients needed for growth. Many people think of soil as simply some "dirt" with maybe a few earthworms. But in reality, it is a living miniature world unobserved by man. Soil is composed of minerals (weathered rock materials), air, water, and a large host of living and dead organisms. Some of the more common members of this organic group include plant roots, bacteria, fungi, insects, and related friends. A teaspoon of soil may contain millions of living organisms.

The typical soil is composed of 5% organic (living and past living organisms), 25% water, 25% air, and 45% mineral materials. In the *desert* climate of the Intermountain West, where low rainfalls limit native plant growth, soils naturally contain less than 1% organic matter!

When we talk of how good a soil is for growing plants, three related but separate items need to be considered: tilth, texture and fertility.

TILTH

Tilth refers to how the particles in the soil mix together forming small spaces for water, air, roots, and micro-organisms. It influences how roots spread and how water moves into and through the soil. Tilth influences a soil's ability to form fluffy seedbed, to hold needed nutrients, and to resist crusting.

If one were to magnify a cross section of the soil, one would find that the water actually coats the soil grains. The air (oxygen needed for the roots to breathe) is found in the spaces not filled with water. This water and air are needed not only for the plant's growth, but also for the insects, bacteria, fungi and other micro-organisms needed to keep the soil's environment favorable for root growth. Some micro-organisms help break down old plant materials, releasing the nutrients to be reused by future crops. Some bacteria assist by fixing nitrogen to fertilize

plants. Many insects and earthworms help by tilling the soils, mixing the particles and organic matter, and improving soil drainage and aeration.

Tilth is easily destroyed by soil compaction. Heavy rainfall and sprinkler irrigation on soils high in clay can compact the soil surface. Traffic moving through the garden, particularly when the soil is wet, can also cause serious compaction. A garden is tilled to break up the soil and reduce the compaction. But tilling a clay type soil when it is wet will form dirt clods, aggravating compaction. Excessive tilling, which totally pulverizes the soils, destroying the open pore space, will also reduce tilth.

Good tilth is slowly developed through root growth and the activity of the many micro-organisms. Man may help this process by yearly additions of organic materials.

TEXTURE

Texture refers to the relative sizes of the inorganic or rock materials in a soil. Sand, the larger particle, is visible to the naked eye. Silt, the medium-size particle, is individually visible under a common microscope. Clays, the smallest rock fragments, are studied only under electron microscopes. The relative proportions of sand, silt and clay is referred to as the soil's *texture class* or texture. References to various types of loam are titles of various textures. For example, a soil containing 65% sand, 25% silt and 10% clay would be called a "sandy loam." Texture can be determined by mechanical analysis or by feel.

Texture plays a key role in how a soil behaves. The term has reference to the soil's stickiness; its water and nutrient-holding capacity; and its drainage, aeration and other properties. Thus the texture will suggest how a garden should be managed. Soils high in clay hold more water and nutrients for crops, but are slower to warm in the spring and may restrict the ease of root spread. Plowing or tilling a wet clay may create hard mud balls.

Sandy soil (in left hand) feels gritty and will brush off, while clay soil (in right hand) feels sticky and leaves the hand dirty.

Clay soils will mold and will form a ribbon when squeezed between finger and thumb. (Photos by David Whiting)

Soil Textural Classes

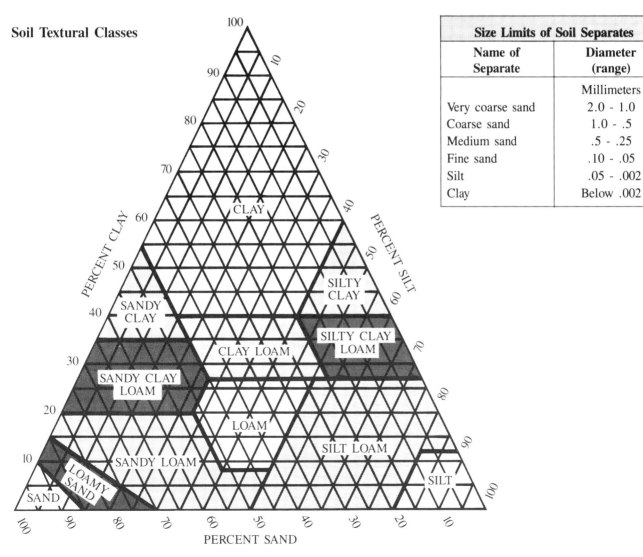

Size Limits of Soil Separates	
Name of Separate	**Diameter (range)**
	Millimeters
Very coarse sand	2.0 - 1.0
Coarse sand	1.0 - .5
Medium sand	.5 - .25
Fine sand	.10 - .05
Silt	.05 - .002
Clay	Below .002

On the other hand, soils high in sand content will warm fast and allow for easy root growth, but it will hold lower amounts of water and nutrients. Vegetables prefer a sandy loam which allows for easy root spread, but a birch tree would be constantly thirsty in this type of soil.

A standard procedure when visiting a garden is to determine the type of soil texture. It is simple to get an idea by feel. Pick up a small quantity of soil and slightly moisten it. Rub it between your fingers. Mold it and play with it. The sand component feels gritty. The clay component feels sticky. Don't be surprised, however, to feel both sand and clay together. Soils high in sand will not mold or form a ribbon when squeezed, while clay-filled soils mold readily when wet. Sandy soils brush off the hands readily; clay leaves the hands "dirty."

Some gardeners try to change a soil's texture by adding soil. This is not at all practical. To illustrate, look at what it would take to change a clay loam to a sandy loam. Since the rooting depth of most vegetables (and lawns) is two feet deep, one would ideally want to change the soil two feet deep. This would take 12 inches of pure sand added over the garden, followed by plowing 24 inches deep, or about 250 tons of sand per 1/8 acre! It can be quickly seen that adding that much sand is not at all practical. Some gardeners try to improve their soil by adding three inches of sand and then plowing eight inches deep. This would give the desired results for the surface soil, but it is still impractical. It would require 12 tons of pure sand per 1000 square feet. Even with the added sand, the more sticky types of clay would still dominate.

Judging Soil Texture by Feel

	SAND	SANDY LOAM	LOAM	SILT LOAM	SILTY CLAY LOAM	CLAY
1. Feel						
Loose, single grained	●					
Somewhat gritty			●			
Gritty		●				
Soft, smooth and floury				●		
Fine texture						●
2. Squeezed moist in the hand						
Crumbles when touched	●					
Forms last if handled carefully		●				
Forms cast (can be handled freely)			●			
Forms cast (wet or dry)				●		
3. Cloddy when dry				●		
Lumps broken easily					●	
Lumps hard to break						●
Lumps very hard to break						
4. Will form a ribbon when squeezed						●
5. Plasticity						
Slightly plastic and smooth			●			
Plastic and sticky when wet						●
Forms heavy plastic: compact mass					●	●

Working with Clay-Type Soils

Clay-type soils have a good ability to hold needed water and nutrients. However, they are slow to warm and dry in the spring, often delaying early spring plantings. They can hold excessive moisture, which fills the soil's normal air space with water, causing the roots to drown. Roots must have oxygen to breath! Clay soils can restrict root penetration and cause surface crusting. Water penetrates the roots slowly, often causing water run-off and soil erosion. In summary, soils high in clay hold water and fertilizers well, but generally have poor tilth.

The best way to improve the tilth in clay-type soils is through yearly applications of organic matter. Gardeners with loam and clay soils should add 2-3 inches of organic matter each year. The clay soil will slowly improve over a period of years. What actually happens in the ground is the lignins and waxes in the organic matter bind the clay particles together and the soil behaves more like a sandy loam.

When I lived in Kaysville, Utah, I gained a lot of sympathy for those gardeners with clay soils. I remembered studying about sticky clay soil in school, but no book description is as vivid as actually gardening in the gummy mess. When the soil was wet it clung to one's feet in globs. One step and shoes became three times their normal size. But with just a little bit of drying the soil surface would crust and crack. Beans would have to find a crack to come up through. In the spring it was difficult to get the garden started. During the rainy springs, the soils would just about get dry enough to work and it would rain again.

I remember my first spring on this garden. The lot had not been gardened in recent years. So I had a tractor come in with a power cultivator on the back. After two hours in the 1000-square-foot garden, the soil was loosened only 4 inches deep! I had a beautiful crop of onions and beets that year, which grew above the soil surface. As each year came along, I could see great improvements in the soil. I never brought in manure, but simply plowed in the garden's plants and lawn clippings.

This soil in Kaysville, Utah is typical of many gardens in the Intermountain West. Being up the street a half mile from an old pioneer brick yard would tell me that I would likely have a powerful clay to deal with. Actually the soil was a sandy clay loam, having twice the amount of sand as clay. But a little bit of clay can become very, very powerful.

Adding sand to a clay-type soil does little to improve its workability. A little bit of clay can overwhelm a lot of sand! In some situations, the clay will mix nicely in between the sand grains to form low grade concrete. Organic matter will do far more than sand.

Another thing to watch for in clay and loamy type soils is compaction. A heavy rain or sprinkler irrigation can greatly compact the soil. Where possible, avoid using impulse sprinklers on bare clay soils. A mulch kept over the surface both summer and winter will help reduce compaction and improve tilth. Walking in and through the garden will compact the soil in the path.

In heavy soils, a raised bed garden system is very useful. Established walkways eliminate compaction from foot traffic in the growing bed. It also allows for better draining and faster warming of the soil in the spring.

With clay soils, care must be taken not to plow or till when the soil is wet. Any type of mixing will create mud balls. A neighbor in Kaysville plowed down his fall weeds into the wet spring soil and made lovely bricks! Three years later he still had many of these brick-like dirt clods in the garden. If the soil is wet enough to mold, it is too wet to plow. Don't be over zealous to get the spring garden planted. A simple wet tilling can destroy a garden's tilth. (In Kaysville, the soil took only a few days of drying and it would become too hard to till dry. A good gardener has to be ready to till when the soil is just right.)

In clay soils, care should be taken to avoid compaction. Organic matter should be added each year. Improvement will come slowly, but steadily, from year to year.

Working with Sandy Soils

Sandy soils warm quickly and resist compaction but they hold less water and nutrients for the plants than clay soils. Thus they have to be watered and fertilized more often. Nitrogen fertilizer leaches easily from the plant root zone with even a slight over-watering.

The best treatment to improve a sandy soil is also the yearly application of organic matter. Organic matter will hold 3 to 30 times more water and fertilizer than sand. Keep the organic matter coming.

SOURCES OF ORGANIC MATTER

Organic matter is just another name for dead plants. It can be pea vines, corn stocks, carrot tops, old flowers, leaves, and so on. Manure is simply plant materials processed through an animal. Compost is plants which are decomposed beyond recognition. Good gardeners keep their eyes open for any readily available, inexpensive sources of organic matter.

Lawn clippings can be used as a mulch to control weeds and to conserve water. Other soft leafy materials, like carrot and radish tops, can also be added to a surface mulch as these crops are harvested. Mulch materials are plowed into the soil at the end of the season. Grass clippings and other soft leafy plant debris are low in lignin and waxes and do not produce long term soil improvement. But with a large quantity of grass clippings added over the course of a summer, some improvement can be seen.

Plow old vines, flowers, and fall leaves into the garden each fall, letting them decay directly in the garden. More bulky materials, like pea vines and cut-up corn stalks which needed to be removed during the summer, should be placed in compost piles. Straw, old hay, sawdust, and other wood chip products can be composted. However, do not compost or plow in diseased plants, or weeds which have gone to seed.

Using large quantities of woody-type products such as sawdust, bark, leaves, straw, etc. can create a nitrogen deficiency. To overcome this tendency simply add some nitrogen fertilizer when incorporating them into the soil. Use 10 pounds of ammonium sulfate (21-0-0) or equivalent per 1000 square feet for each inch of woody materials added.

Making a Compost Pile

Compost is the dark, partially decomposed form of organic matter. It is ready to use when the original identity of the materials it contains is lost.

Composting is a great way to recycle leaves, grass clippings, and other garden refuse. It takes less effort than bagging and hauling it away. Though not high in nutrient value, compost is very valuable to improve soil tilth. It can also be used as a surface mulch to control weeds and conserve water, and it may be used as a peat-moss substitute in container plantings.

Making a compost pile is a technique for speeding the natural decomposition of organic materials. Organic materials are broken down by micro-organisms like fungi and bacteria. During the initial stages of composting, micro-organisms increase rapidly. As the materials decompose, some kinds of micro-organisms predominate; others take over as the process continues.

As the organic matter decomposes, temperatures within a pile approach 140 to 160 degrees at the center. This will kill some of the weed seeds and disease organisms in the hot center section. However, in the cooler sections of the pile such sterilization does not occur.

The fungi and bacteria largely responsible for the breakdown of the organic materials require large quantities of nitrogen. Therefore, adding nitrogen fertilizer or fresh manure is necessary for rapid decomposition. During the breakdown period this nitrogen is tied up and is not available for plant use. It is released, however, when the breakdown process nears completion.

Any type of plant material can be composted. However, do not compost diseased plants or weeds which have gone to seed. Avoid using twiggy materials because they break down too slowly.

Table garbage, grease, fat, and meat scraps can also be composted, but they smell and attract dogs, skunks and other pests. Fats are slow to break down, which greatly increases the length of time required before the compost can be used.

The compost pile should be located out of the way, but near the garden for convenience. Since it needs to be kept moist, a source of water should be nearby. Avoid placing the pile under trees. The tree roots will spread quickly into the moist warm material.

The size and shape of the compost pile is not critical. Generally, piles should be about five feet tall and wide to allow for good heating in the center. Small piles, less than three feet across, will be slow to break down. Some gardeners prefer a single long pile, others like to make several piles as the materials become available. To conserve space, the compost can be contained by wire fencing. Chicken wire or hog fence works well for this. Remember that air and water must get into the pile.

Compost pile construction is usually described in terms of layers. In reality, such layers are not well defined. Layering is not essential, but provides for the quickest and most complete decomposition.

The first layer contains 6-8 inches of coarse textured organic matter. If the material is fine, like grass clippings, use only 2 to 3 inches. Moisten the materials, but do not waterlog them.

Next, add a nitrogen source to feed the working bacteria and fungi. One cup of ammonium sulfate (21-0-0) fertilizer works great for each bushel of material. One or two inches of fresh manure may be substituted. Next, add a 1-2 inch layer of soil. This is the source of the needed bacteria and fungi. Now you are ready for another layer of organic materials. You can firm the layer of coarse materials, but do not compact it. Air needs to pass through the pile to keep it from stinking.

For proper heating and decomposition, the pile should be kept moist but not soggy. A weekly watering may be needed during the hot summer months. Turning the pile will speed the process, but is not necessary unless the pile begins to stink. The pile should be immediately turned if the pile begins to stink or smell of ammonia.

Compost is ready to use when it is dark and crumbly, with much of the original identity of the materials lost. Finished compost should have an "earthy" smell. Normally, composting takes from four to nine months, depending on the materials used and weather conditions.

Manures

Manures are a great source of organic materials for improving the soil. They also contain a small percentage of plant nutrients (fertilizers). The fertilizer value of manure varies greatly. It is dependent upon the type of animal, means of collection, storage, protection from the weather, degree of rotting, moisture content, amount of bedding materials and the means of spread and incorporation.

Typical Nutritive Values of Manures (in percentage of N-P_2O_5-K_2O)			
Animal	N	P	K
Air Dry Manure			
Cattle	1.3	0.9	0.9
Sheep	2.5	1.5	1.5
Swine	1.8	1.8	1.0
Poultry	4.5	3.2	1.4
Rabbit	7.0	2.0	0.5
Fresh Manure			
Cattle	0.7	0.4	0.6
Horse	0.6	0.3	0.5
Sheep	1.0	0.4	1.0
Swine	0.5	0.4	0.7
Poultry	1.0	1.3	0.5

Nitrogen is the most valuable constituent of manure. It is also the constituent most easily lost. The loss occurs through the volatilization of ammonia and through leaching by water. About 50 percent of the nitrogen in manure is available to crops the first year with the balance becoming available in subsequent seasons. To maximize the fertilizer value, plow in the manure immediately after spreading. Manures also contain some small quantities of micro-nutrients.

At 1990 fertilizer prices, the nitrogen, phosphate and potash value of air-dry cattle manure is about $24 per ton. In other words, manures are not too valuable for the fertilizer they contain. But manure is very valuable for the organic matter which improves soil tilth.

The use of manure has a major drawback, that of weed seeds. A pick-up load of manure can contain millions of weed seeds! The straw used for bedding in the stable can also provide weeds. Old manure which has been piled for a year will contain fewer viable seeds. The heat generation during decomposition may kill the seeds in the center of the pile. Manure from horses should be considered to have high weed potential. Manure from dairy cows generally has fewer weed problems.

Heavy application of manures may result in salt problems, particularly if it is fresh. Iron and zinc deficiency problems may be aggravated by the heavy use of manure. The toxic build-up of copper, arsenic, boron, zinc and heavy metals have been associated with over use of manures.

If you have a ready supply of manure, consider using it, but never go out of your way to truck in weeds! Many gardeners buy bagged steer manure, which is advertised as weed free. It is doubtful whether the benefits justify the high cost of the bags.

SOIL DEPTH

Soil depth will influence plant growth. If plants can not achieve their normal root spread, management must adjust to compensate or growth will be reduced. Planting in shallow soils will necessitate more frequent but lighter waterings, frequent fertilizations and lighter plant populatons. Vegetables and lawns generally root two feet deep. Many flowering annuals go to 18 inches, while most fruit crops root to four feet or more.

Soils often change dramatically as the depth increases. This is particularly true among the mountain valleys of the Intermountain West. Along Utah's Wasatch front (the shore lines of old lake Bonneville), for instance the soils show a dramatic change every few feet. Some gardeners will find a sand bar down a few inches. Others go into a hard clay layer quickly. Along many of the bench areas, gravel and rock dominate the subsoils.

Changes from clays to sand and gravel, or from sand to clay, will directly influence the movement of water. Water does not drain readily from clays into sands and gravels. Surface soils will easily waterlog when a clay sublayer is present.

Occasionally a very dense, hard layer of soil, called a hard pan, will prevent root and water penetration. Hard pans are difficult to correct. Shallow hard pans may be tilled up. In some situations, drainage can be improved by punching holes through the hard layer. Make a drain hole for every 25 square feet of garden surface. Tilling repeatedly at the same depth can create a hard pan. To avoid this, alter your plow depth occasionally.

PH MEASUREMENT

The term "pH" refers to the measurement of soil acidity or alkalinity. On the pH scale, a reading of 7 is neutral. A reading less than 7 indicates an acid-type soil. The lower the number, the more acidity is found in the soil. Readings above 7 indicate alkali-type soils. Most plants will have suitabl growth within the pH range of 5.5 acidity to 7.4 alkalinity.

Acid soils predominate in most agricultural areas of the world. Lime (calcium) is routinely added to acid soils to adjust the pH. The amount of lime to add depends on the change in pH desired. Consult your county agricultural agent for details concerning local needs. Since most garden books are written for areas with acid soils, liming the soil is a common fertilizer procedure recommended in those books

But in the Intermountain West with its lower rainfall, alkali soils are more common. The pH in these mountain valleys typically runs from 7 to 8.2. Most common garden plants will tolerate this range, and adjustments in pH are not generally necessary.

Sulfur is used to lower the pH. However, sulfur will not significantly lower the pH if the soil is high in calcium, and soils of the mountain west are typically high in calcium.

The pH will influence the availability of many nutrients. Iron beomes less available for plant use as the pH goes above 7.5. Cultural practices will be your best approach for controlling iron deficiency (see Fertilizers - Iron).

A few crops, like blueberries, flowering southern dogwoods, azaleas and rhodendrons, need an acid soil. The best way to grow these acid-needing plants in alkali soils is to replace half of the soils with peat moss. Acid type fertilizers will also be needed monthly to counter the calcium (lime) in our water, which drives the pH up.

The pH of your soil can be tested by your local agricultural college. This reading is standard in soil tests. The simple pH testers available in local stores or through garden catalogues are designed for acid soils and will not give reliable readings on alkali-type soils.

REGULATING SOIL PH

To lower the pH on alkali soils, use one of the following:

Pounds per 100 Square Feet

To lower the pH on alkaline soils	soil sulfur	sulfuric acid	lime sulfur	iron sulfate	aluminum sulfate
from 7.5 to 6.5	1.5	4.8	6.3	12.5	10.0
from 8.0 to 6.5	3.5	11.2	21.0	29.0	23.5
from 8.5 to 6.5	4.0	12.8	16.8	33.2	26.8
from 9.0 to 6.5	6.0	19.2	25.2	49.8	40.2

All added materials should be thoroughly mixed with the soil for best results.

To raise the pH on acid soils use one of the following:

Pounds per 100 Square Feet

To raise the pH on acid soils	Limestone shell meal	OR hydrated lime	lime	Burned dolomite
from 6.0 to 6.5	10	8	7	9
from 5.5 to 6.5	15	12	10	12
from 5.0 to 6.5	20	16	13	17
below 5.0 to 6.5	25	20	16	21

All added material should be thoroughly mixed with the soil for best results.

Source: University of Idaho Soils Handbook

SALTY SOILS

In the West there are some salty areas, the best known being the Bonneville Salt Flats. Soils with excessive salt content are not suitable for agricultural uses and thus man generally does not put his home and cities there either.

Soluble soil salts move wherever the water takes them. Heavy irrigations leach them down past the root zone, while soil evaporation concentrates the salt on the soil surface. (That is how the salt flats were created.) A white deposit or crust on the soil's surface is an indication of soil salinity. These deposits are usually a mixture of sodium, calcium and magnesium salts. As you travel through the countryside, you can observe these salty areas where the soil does not allow the water to drain through with the salt.

Occasionally a garden may suffer from salt problems. Some of the desert soils are a little high in salt content and irrigation water, which is used and reused over and over again, can become salty. The most common source of salt problems, however, is the use of unnecessary fertilizers. Beans, fruit trees, celery, radishes and strawberries are most sensitive to salt problems.

The symptoms of salt problems include a poor stand, poor seed germination, irregular bare spots in the garden and uneven crop growth. Crop yields can be reduced as much as 25% without any damage being apparent. The tips and margins of leaves die from salt deposited as water is transpired from the leaves. Salt injury is most severe during periods of hot dry weather when water use is high.

Since the same symptoms can be caused by other problems, the best way to diagnose salt build-up is through a soil test by your local agricultural college. If they confirm a salt problem, they will advise you as to special procedures needed based on their measurement of salt, sodium, and pH.

Leaching is the only practical way of removing excess salts. This is effective only if drainage is adequate. Leaching is done by moving water down through the soil, not across the surface. As a general rule of thumb, 6 inches of water leaching through the root zone will take about 50% of the salt. Twelve inches of water will take out about 80% of the salt. Twenty-four inches of water will take about 90% of the salt.

Where salt levels are a routine problem, applying a little extra water in the irrigation will help keep the salts moving through. Irrigating more often can keep the soil moisture from becoming too salty and will decrease the harmful effects of the salt on plant growth.

3
Fertilizers
The Key to Increased Yields

Plants feed on the basic elements carbon, hydrogen and oxygen. And through the process of photosynthesis, they convert these elements into sugars, carbohydrates and proteins. When the gardener supplies these elements to feed the plants, they are called fertilizers. Fertilizers come in many types such as dry granular, liquids, manures, composts, etc.

When a nutrient is in short supply, growth is limited until that nutrient becomes available. Fertilizers are routinely added to supplement those nutrients which are commonly needed. Gardeners need to realize that fertilizers will not correct other growth problems. Adding nitrogen will not improve growth when the phosphorus is limited. Nor will adding fertilizers improve growth when the problems come from poor watering, wind or heat stress, or poor soil tilth.

PLANT NUTRIENTS

Plants have 16-plus common nutrients essential for growth. Carbon (C), hydrogen (H) and oxygen (O) make up 95-99.5% of the plants' physical structure. Carbon and oxygen are supplied by the air; hydrogen comes from the water.

Nitrogen (N), phosphorus (P) and potassium (K) are referred to as the "primary nutrients," being the most significant nutrients applied as fertilizers. Nitrogen is made available through the work of soil micro-organisms from the air and through the decomposition of organic materials. Phosphorus and potassium are provided by the soil and through the recycling of plant materials (organic matter).

The "secondary nutrients," sulfur (S), calcium (Ca) and magnesium (Mg), are generally supplied in adequate amounts by the soil. The "micro-nutrients," those nutrients needed in very small amounts like a few parts per million, include Iron (Fe), Manganese (Mn), Copper (Cu), Zinc (Zn), Chloride (Cl), Boron (B), and Molybdenum (Mo). Micro-nutrients are also provided by the soil and through the recycling of organic matter. Some plants have also been shown to use sodium, cobalt, vanadium or silicon.

The following table summarizes the symptoms of deficiency and excess of the various nutrients. Notice the forms in which the nutrients are absorbed into the plant. Plants take up nutrients as ionic salts. Plants do *not* absorb them as vitamins, proteins, sugars, etc. These organic compounds must be broken down by soil bacteria before they can be used by the plant!

Nutritional deficiencies are difficult to diagnose. Symptoms often overlap and can be mimicked by other growth factors. Crops easily suffer from "hidden hunger"—fertilizer stress causing yield losses but giving no other symptoms.

The unavailability of nutrients to the plant can also cause deficiencies. For example, nitrogen and phosphorus will be held back from plants in cold soils. The soil's pH has a major impact on nutrient availability. Iron is more difficult for a plant to absorb from alkali soils, a typical problem in the Intermountain West. Water is also a factor in nutrient up-take. Again, iron will be less available in wet soils.

Nitrogen, phosphorus and potassium are routinely added as fertilizer. However, soils in the Intermountain West are naturally high in phosphorus and potassium. Iron deficiency is common in Western soils. Zinc deficiency is rarely observed in fruit orchards. The other elements are generally supplied in adequate amounts by native soils.

What Fertilizers are Needed?

For best productivity, gardens need yearly applications of both organic matter (for good soil tilth) and fertilizers to provide needed plant nutrients.

Standard fertilization procedures call for the yearly application of nitrogen, phosphorous and potassium. National brands of "all purpose" fertilizers typically carry about equal percentages of nitrogen, phosphate and potash. Special vegetable and flower fertilizers generally carry slightly higher levels of phosphate. The rate of application is always based on the percentage of nitrogen contained in the fertilizer.

However, soils in the Intermountain West are naturally high in phosphorus (P) and potassium (K). In addition, phosphate and potash applied to the garden as fertilizers, manures and crop residues remain in the soil until used by crops. Soils in the Intermountain area generally do not require heavy yearly applications of phosphorus or potassium.

It is impossible to make any blanket recommendation for fertilizing gardens in the soils of the Intermountain West. Fertilizer application should be based on that garden's cropping history. Gardeners who routinely add compost/manures, or who occasional use a balanced fertilizer, will likely have adequate P and K levels.

Gardeners growing on poor rocky soils, or in a subdivision where the topsoil was removed, or where the soil

Plant Nutrients

Nitrogen, N
Absorbed by plants as: NO_3^- (nitrate) and NH_4^+ (ammonia)
Function in plants: amino acid and proteins.
Deficiency symptoms: a general yellowing and stunting of plant, general reduction in growth of shoots and roots. New shoot growth is limited, thin and woody. Foliage is sparse, yellowish and may develop a orange, red or purple tint. Leaves drop (defoliate) early, beginning with the older leaves. Flower buds formation is greatly reduced and flower buds open late. Bark of trees tint to a brown or reddish-brown.
Effects of Excess: excessive growth. Succulent, overly tender, lush growth. Flower development and fruit maturity may be delayed.

Phosphorus, P
Absorbed by plants as: HPO_4^{-2} and $H_2PO_4^-$
Function in plants: enzymes and energy transfer systems.
Deficiency symptoms: symptoms are similar to those of nitrogen deficiency, making it difficult to clearly define. Leaves color a dull purple or olive green. Fruit is soft, flushed (green ground color) and sharply more acid. Fruits may develop a thicker skin and are poor keepers. Root growth may be reduced. *Phosphorus availability to plants is low in cool soils. Deficiency symptoms are common in the early spring and often correct as the soils warm. The purplish leaves of spring roses and grass are examples of this.*
Effects of Excess: excessive P will promote imbalances with iron, zinc and other micro-nutrients.

Potassium, K
Absorbed by plants as: K^+
Function in plants: metabolic catalysis, enzyme activator.
Deficiency symptoms: growth is dwarfed and thin; length between nodes (stems or leaves) is shortened. New shoots may die back. Leaves show a bluish-green or yellowing tint with margins turning brown or grayish-brown. Plants may tiller (send up an excessive number of shoots). Flower buds are sparse, and tend to open early. Fruits often drop, are small, and variable colored. Ripening can be delayed. Fruits are woody and sweet.
Effects of Excess: salt problems.

Calcium (lime), Ca
Absorbed by plants as: Ca^{+2}
Function in plants: structural component of cell walls, enzyme activator.
Deficiency symptoms: reduces growth in all actively growing areas, like terminal buds, roots, fruit development.
Effects of Excess: salt problems.

Magnesium, Mg
Absorbed by plants as: Mg^{+2}
Function in plants: chlorophyll, enzyme activator, respiration.
Deficiency symptoms: Lack of chlorophyll to form, interveinal chlorosis (yellowing) similar to iron deficiency. Symptoms appear first on older leaves and progress to younger ones.
Effects of Excess: salt problems.

Sulfur, S
Absorbed by plants as: SO_4^{-2}
Function in plants: used in amino acids, proteins, and enzymes.
Deficiency symptoms: uniform chlorosis (yellowing), stunting. Spindly growth is typical of N deficiency.
Effects of Excess: salt problems.

Plant Nutrients (continued)

Iron, Fe
Absorbed by plants as: Fe^{+2} and Fe^{+3}
Function in plants: chlorophyll, enzyme co-factor, cytochromes, oxidases, etc.
Deficiency symptoms: interveinal chlorosis (yellowing between the leaves' veins). Veins remain as thin green lines while the leaves become yellow or even whitish. Fruit is highly colored. Iron deficiency is similar to manganese deficiency and injury of soil sterilant weed killers.
Effects of Excess: toxicity and interaction with other micro-nutrients.

Manganese, Mn
Absorbed by plants as: Mn^{+2}
Function in plants: enzyme co-factor.
Deficiency symptoms: interveinal chlorosis (yellowing) and necrotic (brown) spotting of leaves; symptoms are typical of iron deficiency. Symptoms appear generally throughout the plant.
Effects of Excess: toxicity.

Zinc, Zn (little leaf)
Absorbed by plants as: Zn^{+2}
Function in plants: enzyme co-factor.
Deficiency symptoms: often called *Little Leaf* from its symptoms of small narrow leaves with very short internode spaces (spaces along the branch between the leaves). It looks like an elastic has pulled all the leaves off a branch into a cluster or rosette effect. Foliage may show mottled chlorosis (yellowing) or necrosis (browning).
Effects of Excess: toxicity, imbalance of other micro-nutrients.

Boron, B
Absorbed by plants as: $H_2BO_3^-$
Function in plants: involved in the metabolism of carbohydrates, sugars and polysaccharides; and in cell division.
Deficiency symptoms: loss of terminal buds, necrosis (browning) and malformation of young leaves.
Effects of Excess: toxicity, necrosis of leaf tissue around perimeter.

Copper, Cu
Absorbed by plants as: Cu^{+2}
Function in plants: enzyme co-factor, important for Fe metabolism.
Deficiency symptoms: leaves become yellow or dull bluish-green. Growing points fail to develop or die back. Plants tiller excessively. Seed formation is reduced.
Effects of Excess: toxicity, alters metabolism of other metals.

Chlorine, Cl
Absorbed by plants as: Cl^-
Function in plants: enzyme constituent involved in N metabolism.
Deficiency symptoms: chlorosis (yellowing), necrosis (browning) of leaf tissues, affects water uptake and use in plant cells.
Effects of Excess: salt problems.

Molybdenum, Mo
Absorbed by plants as: MoO_4^{-2}
Function in plants: enzyme constituent involved in N metabolism.
Deficiency symptoms: symptoms typical of N deficiency.
Effects of Excess: toxicity, Cu imbalance.

has been heavily cropped for many years, may find a response to P and K fertilizer.

By way of illustration, consider the soils in the Davis County area (just north of Salt Lake City, Utah). A review of soil tests of gardens in that area shows that about one-third of the gardeners tested have over-applied phosphorus and/or potassium. Overuse of P fertilizer aggravates iron and zinc problems. Overuse of K leads to salt problems. On the other hand, around one-third of the gardens tested would benefit from additional phosphorus or potassium for the heavy feeding crops like potatoes and corn.

To sum it up, soils of the Intermountain West typically need some P and K applied through compost, manures or the occasional use of a balanced fertilizer. But the yearly use of balanced fertilizers high in phosphate and potash are not justified in most gardens in that area.

Where there are questions on the need for P or K, a soil test is recommended. Soil tests are available from local agricultural colleges.

The need for nitrogen fertilizer is different. Soil nitrogen is generally depleted each year by most garden crops and it is readily leached out of the root zone by rain and irrigation. Thus, nitrogen fertilizers are routinely added each season. A good approach would be to make a very light application of nitrogen fertilizer each month through the growing season, particularly on high N-feeding crops like corn, potatoes and asparagus.

SOIL TESTS

A soil test is the best method to indicate whether P or K fertilizer is needed. A soil test is recommended every 5 to 15 years to give the gardener a reading on fertilizer needs. Cost for the test typically run $20 to $40. Soil tests are available through local agricultural colleges. Contact the County Cooperative Extension Service Office for details, mailing address and cost.

What a Soil Test Will Tell You

A standard soil test checks levels for P and K, pH, salt and lime (calcium). The test will indicate whether your garden needs phosphate and/or potash fertilizers. It will indicate the pH and advise if plant growth may be restricted due to salt or sodium problems.

A standard soil test does not check nitrogen levels because it is continuously changing. A standard soil test will not indicate levels of micro-nutrients. It should be remembered that nutrient supply is only one of many factors affecting plant growth. A soil test also will give no information about other problems limiting a garden's performance. It will not indicate if it is over-watered or under-watered, or if there is poor drainage, poor soil tilth, insect or disease problems, weed competition, too much shade, poor vegetable varieties or just neglect. Soil fertilizer tests do not detect toxic chemicals or herbicide residues in the soil.

How to Take a Soil Test

Soil samples may be taken any time of year. The results of a soil test are no better than the sample sent to the lab, so don't shortcut. The sample sent to the lab must be representative of the garden site, so make it a composite of several sampling sites with the sampling depth of 0" through 12" deep. A shortcut sampling is a waste of money.

Steps in obtaining a soil sample:

1. With a shovel, make a 12"+ deep hole in the soil.
2. Throw out this shovelful of soil.
3. Now take the sample by cutting a 1/2" to 1" slice down the back of the hole and place it in a bucket. This sample should include soil from 0 through 12 inches deep. Do not just sample the surface.
4. Repeat steps 1 through 3 at different locations, doing so at least 6 times. This step is important to obtain a representative sample of the garden.
5. Thoroughly mix the 6+ sub-samples. If the soil is wet, spread it on a newspaper and allow it to dry.
6. About 1 pint of the mixed composite sample is needed for the soil test.
7. Send the sample, along with the payment and processing form, to the lab. It takes 10-21 days to get results back.

Gardeners with a soil probe or bulb planter may find them easier to use than a shovel to obtain their soil sample.

In major agricultural areas, private labs also provide soil testing services. These labs often specialize in the major crops of the area. Some labs will report back with a long computer print-out of numbers. But remember, it is not the numbers but the recommendations which are important.

Gardeners will often find home soil test kits available in stores. These kits are designed for eastern acid-type soil and have little reliability with western soil types.

Understanding Soil Test Results

When examining the soil test report, remember that the actual numbers have little meaning in and of themselves. Labs use different testing procedures and different reference points of measurement. Thus, one lab cannot interpret the test for another lab. It is the interpretation of the numbers with their recommendations which is important. Recommendations are based on actual fertilizer test results so always use a local lab which has a local research program to back its recommendations. A lab set up for dealing with eastern acid-type soils will not have the background data on which to base a recommendation for western alkaline soils.

Even within a given area there are differences between labs in the practical interpretation of what is needed. For example, several years ago the University of Idaho had big disagreement between the private labs and the university lab which involved the sugar beet growers. Research by the sugar beet company found that the fertilizer recommendation of the private labs gave the highest yields—they recommended significantly higher fertilizer rates. But the recommendations from the university lab gave the farmers the best dollar return. Under the university fertilizer program, yields per acre were not as high but the sugar content was higher. Sugar beet growers are paid on total sugar, and the dollar return per acre was better with the university's recommendations.

A soil probe makes it easy to extract a sample to 12 inches deep. It is also very handy for checking moisture levels following an irrigation.

TYPES OF FERTILIZERS

A fertilizer is a material containing one or more plant nutrients that can be added to the soil to make the soil more productive. It may be in the form of chemical salts (like common commercial fertilizers) or in organic matter like manures, composts, fish emulsion, etc.

Organic fertilizers—fertilizers derived from the decay of once-living organisms—are preferred by some gardeners. They have the advantage that they help improve the soil's tilth, but the disadvantage that they are bulky to handle and generally low in nutrients. Excessively large quantities may be needed to satisfy the demands of our high-yielding modern production. Difficulties associated with the use of organic-type fertilizers include the introduction of weed seeds, salt problems, heavy metal contamination, and other health hazards. Organic fertilizers must be broken down by soil micro-organisms into the ionic salt form (like the commercial fertilizer) before they can be absorbed by the plant. Thus they are slower to be used by the plant, lasting longer in the soil.

Fertilizers do not come in 100% products. Elemental nitrogen is the gas that makes up 4/5 of air. Phosphorus in its pure or elemental form ignites when exposed to air.

Similarly, pure potassium burns when it contacts water. Fertilizers are compounds of nutrient elements.

All materials sold as "fertilizers" (chemical or organic) must be registered by the Department of Agriculture and carry a guaranteed analysis. The "analysis" refers to the percentage of nitrogen, phosphate and potash they contain. This analysis is always given as three numbers, such as 15-5-10. the first number is the percent of nitrogen, the second is the percent of available phosphate (P_2O_5), and the third number is the percent of potash (K_2O).

Nitrogen fertilizers are primarily made by combining nitrogen from the air with hydrogen to make ammonia. The three most common N fertilizer types include *ammonium sulfate* (21-0-0, 21% N, no P or K, and 24% sulfur), *ammonium nitrate* (34-0-0, 34% N, no P or K), and *urea* (45-0-0, 45% N, no P or K). While all three provide nitrogen for crop growth, there are some subtle differences between their uses.

To understand the fine differences between the nitrogen fertilizers, a little background of what happens to nitrogen in the soil is needed. Plants take up nitrogen as both nitrate (NO_3^-) and ammonium (NH_4^+), but prefer the nitrate form. Soil nitrogen is constantly cycling in its form. Soil micro-organisms break down organic materials, releasing their nitrogen as ammonium and nitrate. The nitrogen in chemical fertilizers is similarly processed into ammonium and nitrate. Soil bacteria convert ammonium into nitrate.

So, when a fertilizer with nitrate is added to the soil, that nitrate is readily usable by the plant. The ammonium in fertilizers can be converted into nitrate, and some may be used directly as ammonium. Nitrogen in other forms, found in the fertilizer, must be processed by soil micro-organisms before it is usable by plants.

Nitrate nitrogen moves readily with water, so it can be easily watered into the root zone, and easily watered down past the root zone (called leaching). Ammonia is held by molecular attraction to the soil particles, and thus is resistant to leaching. Soils high in clay have a strong holding power towards ammonium, while sandy soils cannot hold it as strongly and thus leach easily.

Some of the available nitrogen will be used by the micro-organisms which drive this process. And some of the nitrogen can be lost back to the atmosphere as nitrogen (hence the ammonium smell from a compost or manure pile). This cycling process is continually moving; the activity is slow in cool temperatures and fast in warm weather. Nitrate, preferred by plants, will be in low supply in the spring when soils are cool.

Ammonium sulfate is generally the least expensive fertilizer. Its nitrogen is in the ammonium form. Some of the nitrogen will be used directly by plants, but most will be converted by bacterial activity into nitrate. It waters in easily, and is somewhat resistant to rapid leaching. Like any fertilizer, if over-dosed, it will burn the roots and kill the plant. Ammonium sulfate is generally not used on strongly acid soils, due to the acidifying effect of its sulfur.

Ammonium nitrate fertilizers have both the nitrate and ammonium forms, thus some of their nitrogen is immediately available for plant use. This form is preferred to promote early growth in cold soils. It waters into the soil readily, though it also leaches. Ammonium nitrate is the standard nitrogen base for balanced fertilizer mixes.

Ammonium nitrate or sulfate is the most popular fertilizer for vegetables, fruits and flowers because it is easy to apply. With furrow irrigation, just sprinkle a little down the furrow before watering. With sprinkler irrigation, simply sprinkle it around or over the plants just prior to watering. Do not apply in onto wet leaves and then let it sit or the fertilizer will spot the leaves. If you enjoy tending your garden, it is easy to maintain the desired growth rate of various crops by adding a little here and there. These applications should be light and frequent.

Nitrogen fertilizers based on urea, $CO(NH_2)_2$, are slightly different in their response. Soil bacteria must process the nitrogen into forms usable by the plant. Thus, they take a couple of weeks (in warm weather) to kick into action. This processing time makes nitrogen available over a longer period of time and less resistant to leaching. Thus, they are generally used in premium lawn fertilizers. For the same reason, they would be recommended for the gardener who does not get around to fertilizing very often. Plants will be slower to take off with urea fertilizers in the cool spring.

Phosphorus (P) or phosphate (P_2O_5) fertilizers are obtained primarily from phosphate rock mined from deposits in Utah, Idaho and Montana. The percentage of P_2O_5 contained will depend on the process used to refine the rock.

Potassium (K) or potash (K_2O) fertilizers are primarily derived from lake brines (like the Great Salt Lake) and from rock deposits located in Canada, Utah and New Mexico. It is refined and upgraded into fertilizers like "muriate of potash" (KCl) and "potassium sulfate" (K_2SO_4).

The term "balanced fertilizers" refers to the combining of N fertilizer with the P fertilizer and the K fertilizer. Any combination or grade is possible. Balanced fertilizers with similar percentages of N, P and K are considered general-use or all-purpose fertilizers. Special vegetable or flower fertilizers typically have a higher phosphate level. Lawn food is typically higher in nitrogen. Some balanced fertilizers may also have carrying agents to increase the bulk of the material. There is no magic combination superior to other combinations. The rate of application is always based on the percentage of nitrogen.

Fertilizers vary greatly in cost. Shoppers should compare cost in proportion to the percent of nutrient contained. Bulk fertilizers are usually the best buy. Brand-name fertilizers which are nationally advertised typically run 3-5 times the cost of their generic counterparts. Fertilizers described for a specific use, like Tomato Food or Geranium Food, are also much more costly than a general purpose fertilizer, and may not be any better.

Many of the advertisements for fertilizers are designed to get the consumer to buy a more expensive fertilizer believing that it will give better results. In my opinion, some of these ads border on false advertising! The idea that a special brand of fertilizer will make a lawn and flowers the envy of the neighborhood while the owner fishes all summer is idiotic.

Be cautious of claims that any one brand or combination of N-P-K will produce magical results. Scientific research from agricultural universities across the country has never documented a superior brand of fertilizer. Expensive name-brand fertilizers are not much different from their generic counterparts. The secret is light and frequent applications.

Yes, applying fertilizer lightly and frequently is the key to having a beautiful green lawn, colorful, blooming flowers or a productive garden. The light applications prevent an undesired surge of rapid growth. The frequent applications provide a steady supply of nutrient for even growth. Lawns should be fertilized every 4-6 weeks throughout the season. For simply great results, fertilize flowers and vegetables at least once a month—keep it light and often.

FERTILIZER APPLICATION

Nitrogen fertilizers are water soluble and can be cultivated or watered in readily. Excessive water from rain or irrigation will leach N from the root zone. Nitrogen, for crop growth, is generally added at planting with additional fertilizer added (called side-dressed) during the growing season.

Except for the water-soluble formulations, phosphate and potash fertilizers have little value until cultivated into the soil. They simply remain at the point of application until mixed in. These fertilizers should thus be added just prior to tilling. The fall tilling is an excellent time to plow in P and K, if they are needed.

Fertilizers can be applied by broadcasting, banding, side-dressing or through the water.

Broadcast Application

Broadcast application is simply spreading the fertilizer over the entire garden area. It is fast and easy. Fertilizer is generally applied in the spring of the year, prior to planting. The small "whirlybird" applicators make it easy. Few gardeners are able to hand throw it evenly! Water-soluble nitrogen can be watered in by rain or sprinklers. Balanced fertilizer with phosphate and potash should be tilled into the soil.

The rate of application for a fertilizer is always based on the percentage of nitrogen in the mix. A general rate for vegetables and flowers is 2-3 pounds actual nitrogen per 1000 square feet per year. To figure the rate of application for a specific fertilizer, simply divide the rate (2-3 pounds actual nitrogen) by the percentage of nitrogen in the bag, to get the pounds of fertilizer to apply per 1000 square feet per season. OR, use the table below for the nitrogen percentage closest to the bag.

Standard Application Rates for Garden Fertilizers (pounds of fertilizer per 1000 sq. feet per season)
12 pounds of 21-0-0 (ammonium sulfate), OR
7 pounds of 34-0-0 (ammonium nitrate), OR
6 pounds of 45-0-0 (urea), OR
50 pounds of 5-x-x, OR
25 pounds of 10-x-x, OR
17 pounds of 15-x-x, OR
12 pounds of 20-x-x

Adjustment in the actual rate applied should be made according to crop need and garden history. Be careful not to over fertilize low nitrogen crops like beans, cucumbers, melons, peas, peppers, strawberries and tomatoes. High nitrogen will promote excessive vine growth at the expense of fruiting.

On the other hand, high nitrogen crops such as asparagus, cabbage, carrots, corn, parsnips and potatoes will likely need some extra fertilizer applied during the season to keep them vigorous.

Additional fertilizer will also be needed in intensive garden designs where plant populations are high, where second crops follow the first planting, and where fresh organic matter (like leaves, sawdust, mulch or straw) is added to the soil.

Generally do not use the standard rate all at one time. Crops give better growth with lighter, more frequent fertilizer applications.

Band Application

Band application is where the fertilizer is applied in a band or row to the side of the seed or plant row. It has the advantage that the nutrients are concentrated near the young plant for rapid early development. Band applications use less fertilizer but require more labor to apply. Place the fertilizer in a furrow 3 inches deep. Cover and make the seed furrow 2-3 inches to the side. Do not permit the seeds or plant to come in direct contact with the fertilizer. Use 2-4 tablespoons of a typical garden fertilizer per 10 feet of row.

Fertilizer may also be spot applied to individual plants like tomatoes, cucumbers, squash, etc. Apply about two tablespoons of garden fertilizer to the side of the plant, 3-4 inches deep.

Sidedressing Fertilizers During the Season

Many crops will benefit from what is called "sidedressing" of nitrogen (applying nitrogen fertilizer to the side of the plant during the growing season). High N crops should be sidedressed every 2-4 weeks, as needed, to maintain a healthy green color. Simply sprinkle the water-soluble ammonium sulfate down the furrow or over the surface just prior to irrigation. Use 1/2 pound (about 1 cup) per 50 feet of row. (When using ammonium nitrate, use 1/3 pound per 50 feet). Even low-nitrogen crops, like tomatoes, may be benefited by a light sidedressing applied during fruit production. Be careful not to overdose.

Fertilizer Burn

Fertilizers do not burn plants when applied correctly. But any fertilizer, chemical or organic, if over applied, can cause burn. When a fertilizer (fertilizers are salts) is applied to a soil, the soil moisture moves toward it. The fertilizer (salt), then dilutes and disperses it. Plant burn is caused when moisture is pulled from the tender roots to the fertilizer. The damage is acute. Roots are dehydrated, and the plants are stunted or killed.

The problem can stem from banding fertilizer too close to the tender plant, from uneven applications which over concentrate spots, or from simple gross overdosing. Fertilizing into dry soil can aggravate the problem. Ammonium fertilizers, carrying a relative higher salt content per weight, have a smaller margin of error when over-applied. But, if you burn your plants with fertilizer, don't blame the fertilizer, blame the one who over-applied it.

Special-use Fertilizers

As has been mentioned, ammonium sulfate or ammonium nitrate are good all-purpose nitrogen fertilizers. Urea has the advantage where frequent applications are not possible, and where leaching in sandy soils is a problem. Some special-use balanced fertilizers also need considerations.

Time Release Urea fertilizers (also known as sulfur-coated urea) are used in some of the more expensive lawn and flower formulations. A coating over the fertilizer pellets slows the release of nitrogen over a period of time. Release is based on temperature and bacterial action, with warm temperature speeding the release rate. In theory, they sound great; in reality, the higher cost is not always justifiable. In situations where frequent fertilizer application is not possible, these time-release fertilizers may be helpful.

Osmocote brand fertilizer is another very popular time release fertilizer for specialty crops and potted plants. Most gardeners have seen it in potted plants and nursery stock they have purchased. The round, egg-like pellets are often mistaken for insect eggs. Osmocote is a coated pellet which releases a small quantity of nutrient each time it is watered. This action makes it one of the best fertilizer options, but its high cost makes it prohibitive for general garden use. It is, however, tops for anything growing in a container where the root system is confined and high fertility is a must. In the greenhouse, it can be used as a supplemental feed on hungry crops like fuchsia baskets and poinsettias. At home it can be routinely used in potted plantings, i.e. hanging baskets, patio planters, window boxes and house plants.

Osmocote is available in many combinations for various crops, with a release period of 6 weeks to 9 months. The standard all purpose 14-14-14 Osmocote releases over a 3-month period at 70 degrees. In summertime planters which are watered every day, it will hold for about 6 weeks. Use it as a light feed, supplementing it with water soluble fertilizers when an extra feeding is needed.

Water-soluble fertilizers have a big place in the horticultural industry. They are the fertilizer backbone of large-scale production. Water-soluble fertilizers are those which are added to the irrigation water prior to application. The fertilizer water can be sprayed right over the top of the plants. Water solubles have the advantage of better control over application rate and thus over plant growth. The fertilizer is added to the water in such a light rate that it eliminates the chance of fertilizer burn. Plants can be watered/fertilized twice a week, weekly, every other week, or whatever is needed to push the desired growth. The standard application rate is weekly for young growing plants. If there is a need to push a plant's growth the plant can be fed twice a week. Where there is no need to push growth, the rate can be cut to fertilizing every 2-3 weeks. With water solubles the optimum fertilizer program can be achieved by tailoring the feed to the crops' needs.

Water-soluble fertilizers' disadvantages are their cost and labor intensity. The average gardener runs a risk of failure with these fertilizers because they just do not get it on! Water-soluble fertilizers require the gardener to thoroughly water the soil root zone. Many gardeners fail because they wet the leaves or soil surface only. This is not an adequate feeding. Water the soil! (Some gardeners have the idea that the fertilizer is absorbed through the leaves. Actual research finds that very small amounts of nutrients are absorbed through the leaves.) Another common failure of the home gardener comes in not applying the fertilizer often enough to supply the needed nutrients. A single application supplies enough nutrient to keep a plant going for a few days to a couple of weeks, depending on crop needs. Never get the idea that a couple of applications will keep a crop going for a season. At this light rate, constant reapplication is required.

Miracle Gro, Peters, Shulthz, and *Rapid-gro* are some of the common brands of water solubles on the market. Each year more newcomers come into this market. Hose-on feeders are now readily available to make the job easier. But in large flower beds or gardens, water solubles are still very time consuming. Some gardeners rely on them heavily for spots that need a little extra push. Others find them too labor demanding and too expensive to use as their total fertilization program. Cost of the water solubles can be reduced by purchasing the 25-pound bags used by commercial growers. Dump the bag into a 5-gallon plastic storage container and measure it out as needed.

Root Stimulators are just water soluble fertilizers applied at transplanting. Some brands claim that special vitamins make their product particularly effective. It is interesting to look at the actual research done on these products. Preliminary research has compared the early growth of plants with and without root stimulators. The results were black and white—the plants with root stimulators outgrew those without by 50%+ in just four weeks! However, more in-depth research finds that it is not the Vitamin B in the root stimulator which accounted for the increased growth, but the light water-soluble fertilizer. (Vitamin B definitely has a role in plant growth, but it is just not the magic ingredient in root stimulators.)

The function of root stimulators (water-soluble fertilizers applied at planting) is easy to understand. During spring planting times, the soil temperature is still cold. Nutrients in the soil and from manures, composts or dry fertilizers are naturally less available due to the low temperatures. Using root stimulator fertilizers supply a mild, water-soluble fertilizer solution right into the root zone, with the nutrients in forms for immediate uptake by plants. They work effectively in this situation and are recommended for all transplants and for promoting early growth in gardens. Make two to four applications at 1-2 week intervals. Use them to get flowers to fill in quickly and to get a jump on vegetable transplants. Any water-soluble fertilizer with ammonium nitrate or sulfate as the nitrogen base can be a root stimulator.

Water-soluble fertilizers are easy to apply with the use of hose-on siphon (left) and hose-on feeders (right).

FERTILIZER SUMMARY

Use ammonium sulfate (or ammonium nitrate) as your general use fertilizer. Sprinkle it on lightly and water it in. Nothing can be quicker and easier. Broadcast it lightly over the garden while tilling the soil in the spring. Some gardeners also broadcast it over the garden in the fall as they plow in the fall leaves and garden plants.

Again, ammonium sulfate (or nitrate) is used to side dress corn, potatoes, asparagus and other vegetable crops every 3-4 weeks, as needed to maintain a rich green leaf color. Just remember to make the application light!

In potted plants, hanging baskets, window planters, house plants and potted vegetables, many gardeners prefer the ease of Osmocote. This may be supplemented with water solubles where needed.

To promote rapid growth in the cool spring soils and on new crops of summer vegetables, try a few shots of water-soluble fertilizers. These should be applied every 1-2 weeks as needed. (Plants will respond to the fertilizer in sunny weeks, but not in cold rainy weather.)

Let your transplants have 2-4 applications of root stimulators, or in other words, a water-soluble fertilizer applied at plantings. Try to apply it weekly until the plants begin to size up and fill in.

In the summer, water solubles are good on the vegetables and flowers if they are applied every 2-3 weeks. But to save time, most gardeners generally sprinkle on a little ammonium sulfate and water it in about once a month.

The secret to a great garden or flower bed is not the "special" brand or combination of nutrients used, but frequent light fertilization!

IRON DEFICIENCY

No discussion on nutrients and fertilizers would be complete without covering iron deficiency, the only micro-nutrient deficiency common to the Mountain West. Iron chlorosis (yellowing) is common and potentially serious in many garden plants including fruit trees, grapes, raspberries, roses, junipers, catalpa, silver maples, etc.

Iron chlorosis appears as greenish-yellow leaves with pencil-thin green veins. As the condition worsens, the leaf color fades to yellow, then to ivory white. The veins themselves always remain darker green than the surrounding tissue. In some plants the leaves turn brown around the edges and between the veins. The deficiency may show on a single branch, a side of the plant, or on the entire plant.

Damage from soil-sterilant weed killers has similar symptoms. With soil-sterilant damage the veins and tissue along the veins remain green. With iron chlorosis, only the veins remain green. The symptoms are almost identical, but easy to distinguish.

Most soil in the Intermountain West contains sufficient iron; the chlorosis develops when the iron is unavailable for plant use. This may be due to high soil pH, excessive soil moisture, poor drainage, or the over-use of phosphate fertilizers.

Mechanical problems in the plant may also interfere with the iron moving into the root, up the trunk, out the branches and into the leaves. Problems like root disease, trunk girdling, winter injury, frost injury and other structural damage often account for chlorosis on just a branch, side, or on all of the plant. Plants with iron chlorosis are less able to handle winter's cold than other plants and winter injury will hamper iron movement into the leaves.

Control

The main control of this yellowing is correct watering. Avoid excessive irrigation and avoid irrigation too early in the season. Research suggests that most of the chlorosis seen in fruit crops is due to excessive spring irrigation and/or rainfall. Deep-rooted crops like fruit trees and grapes do not need as frequent irrigation as vegetables or lawns. And most important, they will not need irrigation as early in the season. Correct watering may be the only practical approach in many situations.

Soil applications of iron products are effective but rather expensive. When the soil pH is above 7.5 (and 3/4 of the soils along Utah's Wasatch Front are), the product "Fe Sequestrene 138" should be used. This is a special chelated material for alkaline (high pH) soils, and has shown excellent results in research trials when applied to the soil in the early spring. Applications should be on before May 1st. Applications applied in the summer will generally not take effect until the following spring. One application generally lasts two years. Unfortunately, its high cost makes it rather prohibitive.

On high pH soils, iron products like iron sulfate or other chelates have given poor or inconsistent results in research trials. Again, applications made before May 1st would be best. Just be careful at throwing a lot of money at products which may not give satisfactory results.

Lowering the soil pH with sulfur is helpful in the control of iron deficiencies. However, high pH soils are typically also high in calcium (this lime is what makes the pH high to start with). Lowering the pH on high-calcium soils is basically impossible. The idea sounds good, but does not work in many areas.

On acid soils, iron products like iron chelates and iron sulfates may be helpful. The product of choice here is "Fe Sequestrene 330." It should also be applied in the spring for best results. However, in acid soils, the iron problems are less severe and can usually be corrected with proper soil moisture.

Several new materials are currently under testing for iron chlorosis. Some are applied as a capsule implanted under the bark. Early testing shows some promise for this approach, but the concept of capsule implantations is very controversial among the leading experts.

As a last resort, foliar sprays of iron can give temporary help, often lasting a few days to a few weeks. Follow label directions carefully, since foliar sprays have a strong tendency to burn the leaves. Apply the foliar spray every 10-14 days, as needed. Spray in the evening for best results. Response to foliar sprays varies with crops. Raspberries, for example, readily respond to foliar sprays, while grapes show little response. The product of choice for foliar sprays is "Fe Sequestrene 330."

Other factors contributing to iron chlorosis, like poor drainage, excessive use of phosphate fertilizer, root diseases, etc., should be corrected.

Symptoms of iron chlorosis show as a general yellowing of the leaves with the veins remaining green. Under severe conditions, leaves may bleach to light yellow or white.

Damage caused by soil sterilants show symptoms similar to iron chlorosis, but with sterilant damage, the tissues along the veins remains green. (Photos by David Whiting).

4
Weeds, Mulches and Irrigation

Time spent in the daily care of a garden is in weeding and watering. Neither need to be time consuming. Here are some suggestions to get keep your routine maintenance to a minimum.

WEEDING

It is easier to prevent weeds than to pull them. If you like to pull weeds, skip this section. If you would prefer to grow tomatoes and corn instead of weeds, read on carefully. This section may change your approach to gardening.

Many people apparently like weeds. They give them lots of space, allow weeds to grow rapidly with good feed and water, and they propagate them by allowing the weeds to go to seed.

Weed control can be approached through a style of gardening, not just tilling and hoeing. In an intensive garden design, vegetables are promoted and weeds are suppressed. If you never allow the weeds to get a foothold, you will spend a lot less time weeding.

Never Let A Weed Go To Seed

The number one rule for a weed-free yard is don't let the weeds go to seed. Gardeners often blame the irrigation water for their weed problems, and the water does bring in seeds. But allowing just a few weeds to go to seed will plant far more seeds.

Many gardeners plant weeds by the millions. When a weed is allowed to mature and go to seed, it will return back to the garden thousands of seeds to keep the cycle going. The table gives some of the typical seed production for common garden weeds. To get behind on weeding allows the weed problem to snowball, greatly increasing the total amount of work.

When I lived in Twin Falls, Idaho, we had terrific neighbors who had beautiful, weed-free yards. And how weed free they wanted to keep them was vividly impressed upon me when I moved into the "weedy" house on the block. As we moved in, the neighbors very politely let me know that they expected something to be done with the yard! I kept the yard fairly nice, I thought, but quickly learned how serious the neighbors were about weeds. Early Saturday morning, my neighbor would ring my door bell to let me have back the weed she had pulled in my yard! She did not want it to go to seed and blow into her yard. While this approach is not likely to work on most neighbors, I got the message.

Typical Seed Production of Common Garden Weeds		
Weed	Seeds produced/plant	Viable for
Barnyard grass	7,160	
Curly Dock	29,500	80 years
Dandelion	15,000	
Dodder	1,600	
Foxtail		30 years
Lambsquarter	72,450	
Prickly lettuce	27,900	
Common mallow		20 years
Common mustard	2,700	
Common pigweed	117,400	40 years
Purslane	52,300	25 years
Ragweed	3,380	
Shepherd's purse	38,500	35 years
Leafy spurge	140	
Canada thistle	680	
Russian thistle	24,700	

Taken from the North Dakota Agriculture Extention Circular #116

Pull Weeds While They Are Young, Remove the Weeds From the Garden

The time spent over the season in weeding can be greatly reduced by thoroughly weeding the garden each week, removing the weeds when they are small. Weeds are easy to remove when small by pulling or chopping them out with a hoe. Some weeds, like pigweed, with just a couple of weeks of growth will spread a root system which makes pulling difficult.

Tilling is a common procedure to remove weeds, but each time the ground is tilled, a fresh crop of weed seeds is brought to the surface to germinate. When tilling for weed control, just turn the top one inch of soil. You will not bring up as many ungerminated seeds. This works only if the weeds are very young. After the first month, the amount of weeds germinating slows down greatly.

Remove the weeds from the garden as you weed, not giving them the opportunity to reroot. Many weeds can reroot into moist soil if left on the ground after being pulled.

Irrigation Methods Impact Weed Growth

The method of garden irrigation influences the weed problem. Seeds germinate when they are brought near the soil surface by tilling and watering. Gardeners who furrow irrigate are aware that their weeds grow along the furrow where the soil is wet. Under sprinkler irrigation, the entire soil surface is wet, so weed germination occurs everywhere.

When a garden is under drip irrigation, most of the soil surface remains dry, greatly suppressing weed germination. Drip irrigation also reduces water use by half.

Keep the Garden Small and Manageable

The standard approach to a garden layout, with 2-3 feet between each row of vegetables, gives a lot of land to the production of weeds. Try using close-row block-type plantings. Under this system, weed growth is held back by the dense plant population. The weeds and crop compete for the same space, light, water and fertilizer. Filling the space with vegetables gives the weeds a good challenge.

All unnecessary walkways are eliminated, so the weeding in these walkways is eliminated. With this system garden size can be cut to half that of the standard layout, leaving only half of the area to keep weeded each week. With this system a modest-sized garden can be weeded in just minutes a week.

Prevent Weeds With Mulches

This is the most visible thing that can be done to control weeds. Mulching keeps weeds from getting started. A good mulch eliminates 99% of the weeds, so a yard can be weeded in just minutes a week! See the section on mulches below.

MULCHING TO SAVE WORK

Using a mulch in a vegetable garden or flower bed provides so many benefits that it should be regarded as one of the most valuable of gardening practices. Try to mulch everything, primarily for weed control.

A good mulch eliminates most weeds. Only a few of the more persistent perennials generally push through. Hoeing or tilling, therefore, is not necessary. When an occasional weed pokes through, just pull it. The most difficult weed for many gardeners is field bindweed (wild morning glory). Mulching is even helpful in the prevention of this problem.

The conservation of soil moisture is another important benefit of mulching. A good mulch will reduce the amount of water lost from the soil by half. The moisture supply is kept more uniform, favoring root activity near the soil surface and eliminating problems like Blossom-End Rot on tomatoes. Mulching lessens the compaction and erosion caused by rain and irrigation.

Vegetables thrive in mulched soils. Soil temperatures can be raised or lowered, improving quality and quantity. Gardeners must be alert to symptoms of water, disease and insect problems; however, mulches may hide these from view.

Mulches can be divided into two types: organic (from plant and animal residues) and inorganic (plastics, gravel, stones). Each type has advantages and disadvantages. Some use a combination to capitalize on the advantages of both. Whatever mulching materials are chosen, they should be readily available at little or no cost.

Organic Mulches

If soil improvement is a major goal, organic mulches which improve the tilth should be chosen. When the mulch is tilled in at the end of the growing season, the decaying organic matter helps increase water and air penetration and improves root growth and biological activity for future crops. For each inch of materials plowed in at the end of the season, add 10 pounds of ammonium sulfate per 1000 square feet to aid decomposition and prevent a nitrogen deficiency.

Organic mulches cool the soil. They are ideal for cool season vegetables and many flowers. Carrots, radishes, onions and other root and bulb crops will be sweeter with the cooler summer soil temperatures. Roses and geraniums, for example, will bloom heavier with the cooler soil.

Grass clippings make an excellent mulching material for the garden and flower beds. Apply it only in thin layers, allowing the grass to dry between applications. If fresh clippings are put on too thick (greater than 1/2 inch at a time) they will mat, get slimy and stink. Most germinating weed seeds will be controlled with an inch of dry grass. Throughout the summer, continue to add more layers as the grass is mowed each week. The grass layer dries and shrinks as it breaks down. In the fall, plow the mulch into the soil. Clippings from lawns which have been treated for broadleaf lawn weeds like dandelions should not be directly placed in the garden for three weeks following treatment. They may be composted and applied later.

Use grass clippings on cool season crops, like carrots, radishes, turnips, beets, parsnips, onions, leeks, garlic, peas, cabbage, cauliflower, broccoli, kohlrabi, etc. Cover the walks with it so you don't have to weed them. You may prefer a coarse sawdust mulch on the lettuce, spinach and chard; grass is hard to wash off of these leafy vegetables. Potatoes often are mulched with a thick straw layer.

Coarse sawdust, straw, and compost make excellent mulches and are easy to apply. Simply spread a 2-4 inch layer over the soil surface around the plants, being careful not to cover the plants. Where appearance is very important, like in front-yard flower beds, the commercially packaged mulches on the market are good. This mulching material is generally made up of partially decomposed bark or wood shavings. One cubic yard of mulching material will cover about 160 square feet, 2 inches deep. Sawdust makes a better mulch if it is well rotted. Straw has the disadvantages of looking unsightly, bringing in undesired seeds, and being a potential fire hazard.

You will need to add more mulching material over the old layers periodically in order to keep the layer deep enough to prevent weed growth. Any fresh organic mulch will pull nitrogen from the soil to supply the bacteria which break it down. Be prepared to add a little extra nitrogen fertilizer to compensate. Organic materials are considered fresh if one can identify what they were originally.

Mulches of straw, leaves or pine needles are commonly used around tender perennials to prevent deep penetrating winter frost and to reduce frost heave. Where mulches are used for frost protection, they should be applied after the soils cool in the fall and should be removed in the spring to allow the soil to warm.

Plastic Mulches

A polyethylene film (black plastic) mulch warms the soil and is great for warm season crops. Use it in a large section for cucumbers, squash, melons, pumpkins, tomatoes, eggplants, etc. Due to its warming effect, the garden can produce heavier yields and larger fruits, and production will be advanced 1-4 weeks. It also eliminates most weeding, conserves water and reduces soils compaction.

Black plastic is also the best approach for field bindweed (wild morning glory) control in the garden. Cover the morning glory patch with black plastic and grow warm season crops on this site. Morning glory will find all the holes cut in the plastic for the plants, and any edges it can poke through. But it is far easier to weed these holes than the entire garden area! The black plastic mulch helps

keep it under control in the summer. As fall frosts approach, remove the plastic allowing the whitish morning glory runner to green up in sunlight. Then spray the morning glory plants with Round-up just *after* the first frost to kill the roots. Use plastic mulch the following years to keep the morning glory seeds from germinating.

The soil to be mulched should be prepared as usual by incorporating fertilizers, cultivating and leveling. Drip irrigation is ideal for watering, but furrow irrigation also works well. Place the drip tubes or dig the furrow before laying the plastic.

Use 4-or 6-mil black polyethylene film; 2-or 3-mil (often sold as garden mulch) will not hold up under the high light intensity of the higher elevations of the Intermountain West. Clear plastic warms the soil more than black, but creates a greenhouse for weeds until summer temperatures burn the weeds back.

The plastic is placed over the irrigation furrow or drip tubes. Completely seal the edges from wind (except where the irrigation furrow runs under) by burying all the edges a few inches. Large sheets can be used to spread over several rows, eliminating weeding between rows. Large sheets may need a few shovels of soil placed in the middle to keep the plastic from rippling in the wind.

Planting is simple. Cut small holes where desired and plant the seeds or transplants. Round holes about 3 inches in diameter are better than an "X" cut. They leave no plastic flaps to rub the plants. The plastic warms the soil and the seed will germinate quickly. Be careful not to puncture the drip tubes when planting. To prevent the plastic from rubbing the plant in the wind, place a shovel of dirt around each plant to seal the plastic down.

Summer care is easy. Weeding is almost eliminated. The only areas to weed are the small holes where plants grow. It will not take much to keep these spots weeded. If rain puddles on the plastic, simply prick a few drain holes. Remember that water use will be decreased in mulched areas. Be careful not to over water!

Polyethylene film is broken down by ultra violet sun light. Four- to six-mil plastic will last about a season. Don't plow it under, it will not decay in the soil.

Several brands of "weed mats" are currently on the market. They are used like the polyethylene film and have the advantage that water, from rain or sprinkler irrigation, will seep through. They are great, often lasting for several years, but are rather expensive.

These inorganic mulches which are superior for weed control can be covered with a layer of organic material, like bark, to enhance their beauty.

CHEMICAL WEED CONTROL

Weed control with herbicides (weed-killing chemicals) is a complicated science. Herbicides would be better understood if they were called plant killers instead of weed killers; they cannot tell a flower or vegetable from a weed.

Herbicides function in different manners. Non-selective herbicides are effective against most plants. Selective herbicides work only on a specific plant family or group and not on others. Pre-emergent herbicides work in germinating seeds. There are no herbicides which control weeds across the board but are also safe on desired plants.

Another complicating factor in the home use of herbicides is the vast variety of different plants in the same small area. Farmers have only one kind of plant in a field covering several acres or square miles.

When using a herbicide, care must be taken to consider its effects on all the desired plants in the area to be treated and in adjacent areas where the chemical could leach or drift. Consideration must be given to the varieties of weeds to be killed. Consideration must be given to the future use of the area; so the herbicide does not interfere with the next crop to be planted. And of course, the herbicide must be safe to use around homes and edible commodities. With all this in mind, only *Treflan, Dacthal,* and *Round-up* are left for use around the vegetable garden.

Treflan

Treflan (Trifluralin) is a pre-emergent herbicide used to control seed germination. It is widely used in commercial vegetable production and on transplanted flower beds, perennials and ground covers.

Treflan must be incorporated soon after application. It can be tilled or lightly raked into the top 2 inches of soil, or watered in. Once it is activated, the soil cannot be tilled or plowed. When properly applied, Treflan will generally check seed germination through the summer. Residues can interfere with sensitive crops like spinach, beets and other root crops for 12 months after application.

Treflan is effective to prevent seed germination of barnyard grass, annual bluegrass, bromegrass, carpet weed, chickweed, crabgrass, field bindweed (wild morning glory), foxtail, knotweed, kochia, lambsquarter, pigweed, purslane (portulaca), russian thistle, sandbur, and others.

Treflan can be used on some vegetables and not on others. But it can *not* be broadcast over the garden. Each row of vegetables must be independently considered! And don't forget about what crop may fill in that space later in the season.

Treflan can be used on beans, carrots, celery, collards, garlic, kale, okra, peas, and turnips before seeding. It can be applied to transplants of broccoli, brussel sprouts, cabbage, cantaloupes, cauliflower, cucumbers, melons, peppers and tomatoes.

Treflan can be used in both the vegetable garden and the flower bed and it is very helpful in suppressing seed germination. But it will not control growing weeds, so the treated area must be weed free when applying it. It does not control all weeds, but does help on the pigweed, purslane and morning glory seed—common garden weed problems. Be careful not to overdose the application or suppression in crop growth will occure.

Dacthal

Dacthal (DCPA) is another pre-emergent seed control herbicide, similar in action to Treflan. It must be watered into the soil to activate it. Many gardeners are disappointed in the results of Dacthal for it only checks most weed seeds for about 6 weeks.

Dacthal is effective in controlling the seed germination of crabgrass, carpet weed, dodder, foxtail, ground cherry, lambsquarter, pigweed, purslane (portulaca), sandbur and others.

Dacthal can be used on broccoli, brussel sprouts, cabbage, cauliflower, garlic and onions at planting or transplanting. It can be used on beans, collard, kale, mustards and turnips at seeding. It can be used on lettuce after the crop is up. It can be used on cucumbers, eggplants, melons, peppers, squash, and tomatoes at transplant. It can be used on strawberries in spring application prior to first blooming.

Round-up

Round-up (glyphosate) is not registered for use directly in the vegetable garden, but it can be used around the garden and during the off-season.

Round-up is a non-selective contact herbicide. It is effective on most non-woody plants. It must be applied to the leaf or other green tissues, and is translocated in the plant to the root system. It has no soil action and is not taken up by roots. In fact, dirt will neutralize it.

When mixing Round-up, be sure to use culinary water. The dirt in secondary (irrigation) water can neutralize it. Freezing will also inactivate Round-up.

Probably the biggest use of Round-up around the garden is on perennials like wild morning glory. It is very effective in wild morning glory in the fall *when applied just after the first fall frost.* Summer applications are spotty in effectiveness.

IRRIGATION

From the plant's point of view, water is life. Plant tissues are 65-95% water. Water is a required component of photosynthesis. It is the solvent for chemical activity. It is the plant's internal mode of transportation. It also maintains the plant's turgor (ability to stand and hold its leaves up), and it is the plant's cooling system.

In modern agriculture, the water use of major crops can be measured to 1/100 of an inch of water per day. As irrigators, gardeners don't use such sophistication. But it should be understood that water management will directly impact yield and quality of the produce.

As the water use in any given water district is measured, it is easily seen that there is a lot of improvment needed in irrigation management. Studies with the Salt Lake Water Conservative District suggest that gardeners use twice the amount of water required to maintain local yards and gardens. In your own neighborhood, there are probably neighbors who chronically have dry lawns and others who never seem to turn the water off.

On more progressive farms, computer sensors and modeling programs guide the farmer in his irrigation. Here farmers have been able to significantly reduce their irrigation costs. Another interesting outgrowth of this state-of-the-art research is the significant improvement in yields and quality with careful water management.

Over watering slows root activity. Overly wet soils do not have the soil oxygen necessary for proper root functioning. Under acute conditions, the root system shuts off, and the plant can wilt! This water-logged/wilting response is often mis-diagnosed as a lack of water. Over watering will also slow or stop seed germination, promote many diseases and lead to softer fruits and lower yields.

Symptoms of water deficiencies are easier to observe. Leaf color often changes subtly to yellowish or grayish hues. Leaves flag (look droopy), roll, wilt, or even drop. Fruit produced under water stress will be more stringy and tough, and fruit may fail to set.

Gardeners should know that a little understanding and care in irrigation practices will not only cut their water bill but also enhance the quality of their produce.

How Much and How Often

As water is applied to a soil, it can run off, evaporate, or soak into the ground where it can be used by plants and soil micro-organisms. Run off can be a serious problem causing water erosion and pollution. Evaporation is high when sprinklers are run in the heat of the day, with excessive pressure, or in windy weather. Whenever more water is applied than the soil can hold, it will leach through the rooting zone. This leaching takes the nitrogen fertilizer with it and can be a pollution problem. Where soil conditions prevent leaching of excess water, the soil waterlogs.

As water soaks into a soil, it first fills the pore spaces, the space between the soil particles. When the pore spaces are filled with water it is called *saturation*. If you were to take a handful of soil at saturation you could see the water glisten in the sunlight. If soil remains at or near saturation for too long, generally more than 24 hours, root activity is slowed or stopped. The roots must have oxygen to function. Plants can wilt from lack of water being taken up by the roots.

Gravity and soil capillary action move the water down and out. *Field capacity* is the term which describes that point when excess water has moved out of the pore spaces, allowing air to return. The remaining water coats the soil grains and is held by molecular attraction. The quantity of water a soil holds at field capacity is called *water holding capacity,* and it varies with the soil's texture and organic content.

The soil's water can evaporate from the surface and be used by plants and micro-organisms. The point where a plant wilts beyond recovery is called the *permanent wilting point.* Water needs to be re-applied before the soil reaches this point. At the permanent wilting point, about 50% of the field capacity water is remaining but the plant cannot extract it, and the soil will feel dry.

Soils vary in their *water holding capacity.* Soils very high in clays can be slow to drain from *saturation* to *field capacity* and in some situations this can interfere with root activity. On the other hand, sands have a low *water holding capacity,* restricting plant growth unless water is applied often. The addition of organic matter will improve a sandy soil's water-holding capacity.

Plants use the same amount of water whether in sands, loams or clay-type soils. The difference comes in how much water to apply and how often. When properly managed, sandy soils do not use more water that loams; they just have to have it in smaller amounts more often. The following table gives the typical water demands for various soil types.

Simply stated, the typical summer-time garden or lawn on a sandy soil will need 1 inch of water every 3-4 days. Sandy loam gardens will need 1 1/2 inches of water every 4-6 days. Gardens with loams and clays will need 2 inches of water every 6-8 days.

Now you may need to adjust for non-typical situations. Some of the finest sands cannot hold enough water to go 3-4 days. Adjust the interval and amount accordingly. Rocky soil may likewise need some adjustment in the interval and amount. Shallow or extremely hard soils will need adjustments due to the shallow rooting depth. Simply adjust the figures to fit your own soil, remembering to give 1/4 inch of water for each day in the cycle. If you have to water every 2 days, apply 1/2 inch of water. If you have to water every 3 days, apply 3/4 inch of water. If you have to water every 4 days, apply 1 inch, and so forth. Just spread the waterings as far apart as possible.

Irrigation Summary by Soil Types

	—Soil Texture—		
	Sandy	Sandy Loam	Loams & Clays
Inches of water held per foot of soil (field capacity)	1"	1 1/2"	2"
Plants can use about 40-50% of this water.			
Inches of water usable by plants per foot of soil (water holding capacity)	1/2"	3/4"	1"
Vegetables and lawns typically have a rooting depth of 2 feet in which they can take-up water.			
Inches of water available for vegetables and lawns with a 2-foot rooting depth	1"	1 1/2"	2"
Amount of water to apply during each irrigation	1"	1 1/2"	2"
During typical summer weather our vegetables and lawns use about 1/4 inch of water per day.			
Typical interval between summer irrigations for a crop with a 2-foot rooting depth	3-4 days	4-6 days	6-8 days

How Irrigation Would Change if Root Depths Were Different

If soil condition only allowed roots to penetrate to 1 foot, the irrigation pattern should be:

inches of water	1/2"	3/4"	1"
every	1-2 days	2-3 days	3-4 days

On crops with a 4 foot-rooting zone, like fruit trees, the water pattern should be:

inches of water	2"	3"	4"
every	6-8 days	8-12 days	12-16 days

Wind and the state of plant growth are the other factors which will require adjustments from the typical. During windy periods, a lot of moisture is pulled from the plants and soils. Water use can increase significantly. The frequency of irrigation may need to be increased to compensate. In the mountain west, the southerly summer winds are usually very low in humidity, drying plants fast. The daily temperature fluctuations average out without requiring major adjustment, except in long-term temperature extremes.

Water use by a plant increases as the plant grows and matures. It starts out low, with a correspondingly limited root system. Water need and root spread steadily increase, with water use peaking at the time of flowering and fruit development. As the crop progresses through maturity, water use often cuts back dramatically; vegetables are generally harvested before this cut back period is reached. Water stress during the blooming/fruiting period is common in some crops. For example, corn will fail to pollinate fully because of water stress, leaving gaps in the ear.

With early season and late season watering, the interval between irrigations should be extended, but the amount to apply should remain the same as for the summer irrigations.

Some sign posts along the way to judge specific water needs include the following:

Lawns are easy to judge. As the lawn begins to dry, footprints show up more distinctly. The grass blades are not as fast at returning to their upright position. One of the best signs is to watch the color. It subtly changes to a more grayish cast. As the water need becomes more critical the lawn becomes more gray and dry looking, and then turns to a dry yellowish hue. Water should be applied at the first sign of gray-green. On a hot day, the lawn can begin burning in just a few hours at this point.

Beans are a good measuring tool of watering needs. As the plants begin to call for more water, the leaves turn a darker color. When the water supply is a little short, the developing bean pod will pollywog, that is begin to develop on the top half but fail to fatten up on the bottom, giving a pollywog shape. Beans will also fail to bloom, or blossoms will drop in response to water stress. Potato vines will also darken with the need for irrigation.

Some gardeners prefer to water a little each day. This practice should be avoided. Frequent light irrigation have been found to significantly decrease the quality and yield potential. It also encourages weed and disease problems.

Furrow and Flood Irrigation

Irrigation methods are dictated in part by how the water is delivered. Gardeners who can water on demand, watering any time they want, have the best options. If you are in a water district which is voting for pressurized irrigation systems, go for it!

The old standard type of irrigation is running the water down furrows or allowing it to flood over the surface. This method does not require any special equipment. Ditches are dug to bring the water to the desired spot. Furrow and flood irrigation require that the land have a very gentle slope and be free of dips and high spots. Federal *Non-Point Source Pollution* laws give very restrictive guidelines on the cleaning and control of run-off irrigation water. However, little has been done in enforcement due to the impracticality of the law.

In furrow and flood irrigation, water distribution is rather uneven. The top of the row always gets significantly more water. Management skills for this form of irrigation suggest that the water should reach the bottom of the row in 1/3 of the irrigation time, with the water flow being reduced at this time to decrease run-off.

Furrow and flood irrigation is commonly used where no other options are available. For many gardeners the water is delivered in a ditch at a preset time for a preset duration, and management options are limited.

Some gardeners have good success with basin irrigation. Here a basin or dike is filled with water.

Sprinkler Irrigation

Sprinkler irrigation has the advantage that water distribution is more even than with furrows. With good management, water use will be 1/4 less. The water must be under pressure. Those who have pressurized irrigation water are fortunate. Impact (rainbird-type) heads are most popular for crop irrigation, being more resistant than other sprinkler systems to plugging. Sprinkler irrigation systems are the easiest to manage.

With sprinkler irrigation, water measurement is easy. Just place some straight-sided cans out and collect the water. It is easy to see when you have 1 or 2 inches. If your water pressure is consistent, timers are helpful to turn the water on and off. Set out the cans to measure the amount of water applied and adjust the timer accordingly. Each circuit may require a different running time to apply the correct amount of water.

In sprinkler design, some overlap of circles is required. In a garden setting with plants at varying heights there may be better distribution with 100% overlap. Sprinkler heads must be serviced and must be maintained at true vertical position to maintain the correct distribution pattern. To avoid wasting water, avoid watering during the heat of the day, avoid watering in windy weather, and adjust the pressure down to prevent the sprinkler heads from producing a mist.

Sprinkler irrigation has some disadvantages. The entire soil surface is wet, allowing for weed-seed germination everywhere. The wetting of the foliage can spread disease organisms and the wet foliage allows for diseases to develop. Water on maturing tomatoes and fruit can cause skin splitting.

Drip Irrigation

Drip irrigation systems have many advantages. The soil surface stays dry, reducing weed germination. Plants stay dry, and thus foliage diseases are rare. Water use is cut 30-50%. Gardeners who use culinary water may find this savings a real plus. With drip systems, there can be more control of the water application on individual crops. For example, beans and corn can be given extra waterings during their blooming periods.

Drip systems have some strong disadvantages also. They plug easily, and the crop can be damaged if the plug isn't discovered immediately. Drip systems are also costly, in comparison. Some have even had plugging problems in dew-hose and bi-wall drip systems using culinary water. Filters are available, but it is rather expensive to clean up irrigation water for drip use.

Some gardeners have had good experience with a type of drip tube called the "spray and soak" hose. It is a poly-canvas type tube. Where it is buried under mulch, it lasts 3-4 years. It can be cut into any desired length up to fifty feet, and connected with standard hose fittings. There are few problems with it plugging, even with secondary water systems. Drip systems can be connected to a timing clock, making watering automatic.

Greenhouses use a lot of spot emitters, where water is supplied by spaghetti tubes to emitters in each pot or hanging basket. The system has some application to home owners on patio planters, if a really clean culinary water system is available.

Water Conservation

As the population grows, the need for water increases. Water is becoming one of the nation's most valuable resources. Large tracts of good farm land could be developed in the West if the water was available. Water conservation topics surface in dry years, but conservation should be considered every year. By way of review, here are some things that can be done to reduce water use:

Apply the correct amount of water. The natural tendency is to over-irrigate.

Use soil mulches to reduce soil evaporation.

Sprinkler irrigation reduces water use over furrow and flood methods. Drip irrigation reduces water use over sprinklers.

Maintain the irrigation system for efficient water distribution. Reduce water pressure to prevent misting, which wastes water.

Water in the morning or evening when temperatures are cooler. Avoid watering in windy weather.

Control weeds. Save the water in the soil for the crops.

5
Garden Layout and Planting

The Art of What Goes Where

There are no magical rules as to what crops can be planted next to other crops. It is an art, however, to arrange the vegetables to keep the space filled through the growing season. This is challenging, and even more so for some gardeners who change their layout a bit each year to make room for new varieties and to give the family a variety in the produce grown. Always plan your garden on paper first, making sure that you can fit it all in. Here are some guidelines to consider in a garden layout.

GARDEN LAYOUT

A garden should be located in full sun, and away from the root system of large trees. In small subdivision lots, the garden may need to be divided into sections to get away from shady areas. As a rule of thumb, leaf and root vegetables (lettuce, spinach, chard, beets, carrots, radishes, turnips, parsnips, onions) can get by with a minimum of six hours of good sun a day. A bit of cooling shade during the summer heat may actually be beneficial in warmer valleys. Those crops from which fruit is picked (tomatoes, peppers, eggplant, corn, melons, cucumbers, squash, beans) require full sun for good production.

The direction to run rows is based on what is best for watering and the utilization of space. It actually makes little difference from the sun's point of view. Popular theory recommends that the rows run north to south so the sun can get to both sides of the row each day. Others feel the rows should run east to west, allowing the broadside of the crop row full sun.

However, in solar design principles, a coldframe or covered raised bed (used to extend the growing season) should run from east to west to maximize solar energy input.

Perennials, like asparagus and rhubarb, should be placed on the edge of the garden or elsewhere in the yard so as not to interfere with plowing.

Root crops, which stay in the ground for winter storage (carrots, parsnips, leeks), should be placed along the side so as not to interfere with fall plowing. If you have semi-permanent trellis poles for beans and cucumbers, they likewise should be placed at the edge of the garden.

Corn must be planted in blocks for good pollination. Wind moves the pollen from the tassels (male flowers) to the silks (female flowers). Three rows wide is considered a minimum, but pollination will be more complete with a block four or five rows wide. The blocks need not go the full length of the row. For example, a corn patch 5 rows wide, each 20 feet long, could have the first 10 feet of the rows for early corn, the next 5-foot section for the second crop and the last 5 feet for the third crop.

The vine crops (cucumbers, squash and melons) also can be planted in a block. The various vine crops will cross pollinate within their kinds, and the squash and pumpkins readily cross-pollinate. But this crossing will not influence the fruit of the growing crop, it only affects the seed. When you get a freak fruit on a vine crop, its from a bee that strayed into the seed field last year.

Crop Rotation

Crop rotation sounds good in theory and is practiced by commercial growers for disease control, weed control and soil tilth. In a commercial farm rotation program, large fields alternate crops on a 4-year minimum cycle. Grain crops play a key roll in the rotation.

When it comes to home gardens, rotation sounds good but has little practical application. In the smaller area of a garden, soil tilth can be improved each year by adding organic materials to the entire garden area. Since few of the commercial weed killers are used in the multi-cropped garden, rotation for weed control has no application. However, disease control remains a primary concern to the gardener.

In terms of rotation for disease control, vegetables are grouped by susceptibility to soil-borne diseases. The primary group, with like soil-disease problems, includes tomatoes, peppers, eggplant, potatoes, watermelons, cantaloupes, cucumbers, squash, pumpkins, beans, peas, raspberries and strawberries. This one group in the rotation programs occupies a majority of the garden space. To plant no members of this group in or near the same spot for 4 years is impractical, if not impossible.

In theory crop rotation sounds good, but in reality it has little application for the small garden. Where soil diseases become a problem, crops must be rotated or diseases can be suppressed by fumigating the soil with Vapam.

Companion Planting and Successive Cropping

Part of the art of gardening is known as *companion planting* and *successive cropping*. Companion planting refers to the growing of two crops in the same area. Successive cropping refers to the planting of a second crop following the harvest of the first crop, in a given season. For example, rows of spring peas can be alternated with rows of vine crops (cantaloupes, watermelon, squash, etc.). The peas are harvested early summer, giving their space for the vine crops to spread.

Leaf lettuce and cole crops (broccoli, cabbage, cauliflower, etc.) can be inter-planted in the same row. The quick-maturing lettuce is harvested out, giving their space to the cole crop to mature. Just be careful not to accidentally pull the cole crops with the lettuce.

In companion planting, the two crops should be compatible in both water and fertilizer needs. Some magazines talk of companion planting corn with pole beans, allowing the beans to use the corn to climb on. This is a questionable recommendation. For maximum production, corn is a high-nitrogen crop and does not like the competition for the sun's light. Beans are a low-nitrogen crop. Yields would be reduced, as compared to each crop being grown separately under its optimum cultural practices.

Organic gardeners talk of companion plantings for insect control purposes. However, scientific research has not found this helpful. While marigolds or garlic will not be attacked by Mexican Bean Beetles, they provide nothing other than camouflage; they don't function in the environment to protect the neighboring bean plant.

For maximum production in limited space, rely heavily on successive cropping. Immediately replant radishes, lettuce, spinach, beet greens, etc. throughout the summer, as each short row is harvested. In the warmer areas of the Intermountain West, spring peas could be replanted with late corn, beans, or fall broccoli, cabbage and cauliflower.

CLOSE-ROW PLANTING VS. TRADITIONAL ROW SPACING

The traditional garden layout calls for a plant row, then a walkway or path, and back to a plant row, across the garden. The spacing between the rows is often set to accommodate the use of a tiller for weed control. Some gardeners prefer to use two plant rows, then a walk. Where space is limited, a close-row block-type planting system is preferred. Close-row block planting also reduces weeding!

In the close-row block system (sometime called equal-distance planting) all unnecessary walks are eliminated. Crops are planted in blocks, with an equal distance to the neighboring plants in all directions. It's easier to think of as planting in rows, but moving the rows closer together. For example, carrots can be thinned to 3 inches apart within the row, with the rows 3 inches apart. This fits a standard 24-foot row of carrots (96 carrots) in a block 3 feet by 2 feet.

Kitchen garden vegetable areas are well suited to the close-row block system. The gardeners plant a bed 36-48 inches across; they can reach across the planting beds from the pathway along each side. The rows run across the box. Depending on the crop, the rows are spaced 3 to 18 inches apart (see Vegetable Planting Guide). The wider spacings listed for block planting are the standard for average soils. The narrower spacings listed are for the advanced gardener on improved soils.

Some garden sites would not be suited to this block planting system. For example, a garden site on rocky soil or where irrigation water is available only once a week would not be suitable to maintain this higher plant population.

Vegetable Planting Guide

Vegetable	Traditional Spacing		Close-row block spacing plant to plant*	planting depth	Days to Germination	Typical Days to Harvest
	in row	between rows				
Beans	4"	18-36"	6" or 4 x 12"	1"	6-14	60
Beets	3"	15-36"	3-6"	1"	7-10	60
Broccoli	18"	30-36"	18"	1/2"	3-10	65T
Brussel Sprouts	18"	30-36"	18"	1/2"	3-10	85T
Cabbage	18"	30-36"	18"	1/2"	3-10	85T
Cantaloupes	24"	48-60"	24-36"	1"	3-12	85
Carrots	2"	14-36"	2-3"	1/4"	10-17	70
Cauliflower	18"	30-36"	18"	1/2"	3-10	55T
Celery	8"	24-36"	6-9"	1/8"	9-21	100T
Chard, Swiss	6"	18-36"	6-9"	1"	7-10	60
Corn	9"	36"	12 x 30"	1"	6-10	80
Cucumbers	24"	48"	12-18"	1"	6-10	55
Eggplant	18"	30-36"	18-24"	1/4"	7-10	60T
Garlic	4"	16-36"	3-6"			90
Kohlrabi	4"	18-36"	7-9"	1/2"	3-10	50
Leeks	4"	16-36"	3-6"	1/2"	7-12	120
Lettuce, head	14"	24-36"	10-12"	1/4"	4-10	90T
Lettuce, leaf	6"	18-36"	6-9"	1/4"	4-10	60
Onions, dry	4"	16-36"	4-6"	1/2"	7-12	110
Onions, bunching	2"	16-36"	2-3"	1/2"	7-12	60
Parsnips	6"	18-36"	5-6"	1/2"	15-25	70
Peas	2"	24-36"	4-6" or 3 x 8"	1"	6-15	65
Peppers	18"	30-36"	15"	1/4"	10-20	70T
Potatoes	12"	30-36"	10-12"	4"		125
Pumpkins	24"	48-60"	36-48"	1"	6-10	100
Radish	2"	14-36"	2-3"	1/2"	3-10	30
Spinach	4"	16-36"	4-6"	1/2"	6-14	40
Squash, Summer	30"	48"	30-36"	1"	3-12	50
Squash, Winter	24"	48-60"	36-48"	1"	6-10	100
Tomatoes	30"	48-60"	24"	1/4"	6-14	65T
Turnips	4"	16-36"	4-6"	1/2"	3-10	50
Watermelons	24"	48-60"	24-36"	1"	3-12	85

* Use wider spacings for average soil; closer spacings are for advanced gardeners on improved soils. T = days from Transplant.

Close-Row Block Planting Kitchen Garden

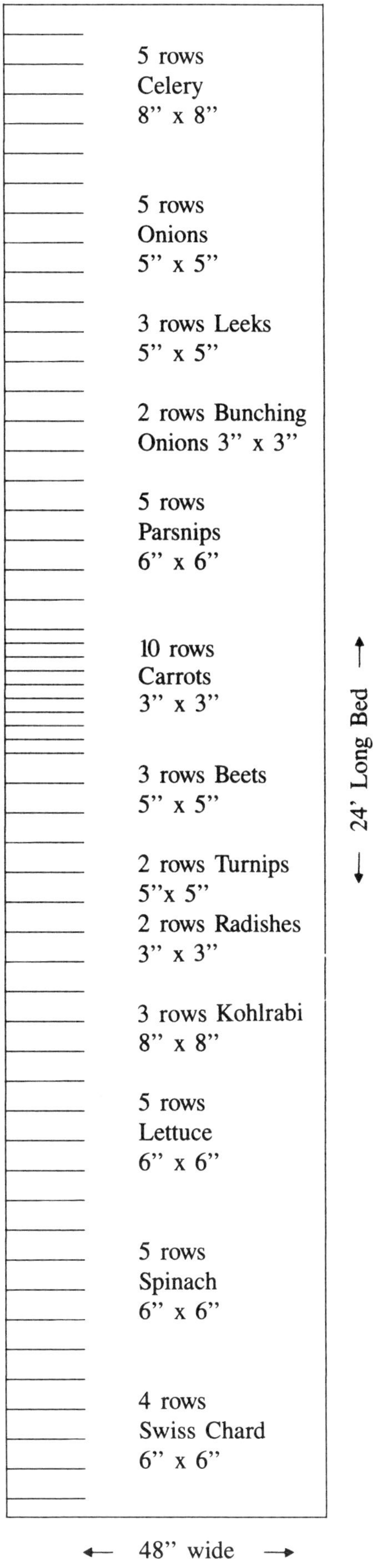

Size 24' x 4' = 96 square feet

5 rows
Celery
8" x 8"

5 rows
Onions
5" x 5"

3 rows Leeks
5" x 5"

2 rows Bunching
Onions 3" x 3"

5 rows
Parsnips
6" x 6"

10 rows
Carrots
3" x 3"

3 rows Beets
5" x 5"

2 rows Turnips
5"x 5"
2 rows Radishes
3" x 3"

3 rows Kohlrabi
8" x 8"

5 rows
Lettuce
6" x 6"

5 rows
Spinach
6" x 6"

4 rows
Swiss Chard
6" x 6"

← 24' Long Bed →

← 48" wide →

Compare this with the same garden in traditional spacing—cutting space need and thus weeding to 17% of the traditional layout.

Beds are mulched to conserve water and control weeds with grass clippings or sawdust.

Individual short rows will be replanted through the summer as crops are harvested.

Kitchen Garden with Traditional Row Spacing
Garden size 27½' x 20' = 550 Square Feet

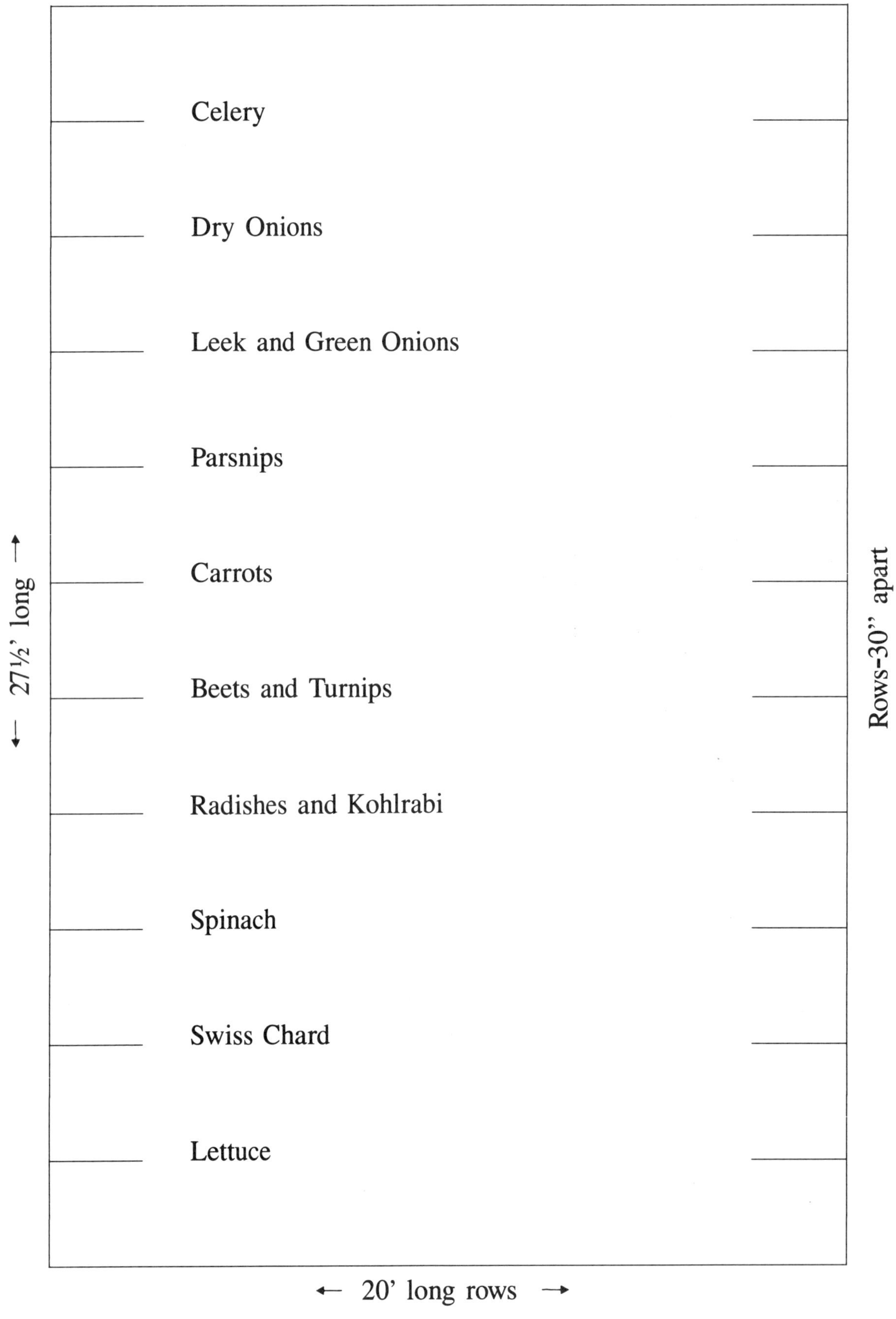

Celery

Dry Onions

Leek and Green Onions

Parsnips

Carrots

Beets and Turnips

Radishes and Kohlrabi

Spinach

Swiss Chard

Lettuce

← 27½' long →

Rows–30" apart

← 20' long rows →

3' x 10' Block 14 Peppers & Eggplants	2' x 8' Block 4 Tomatoes/cages

Walk (left)   Walk (right)

1' x 10' Block 10 Cucumbers/trellised	2' x 8' Block 4 Tomatoes/cages

Walk

Block 6' x 20'
1 Row Squash
1 Row Watermelon & Cantaloupe

Walk

Block 15' x 20'
5 Rows Corn
36" between rows
9" between plant

*Do not crowd corn or
yields will be hurt*

Walk

Block 4½' x 20'
4 Rows Peas, followed by 3 rows of
Cabbage, Broccoli & Cauliflower

Walk

4' x 20' Block
Potatoes on 12" x 12" center
mulched with straw

Walk

Pole Beans

Walk

Pole Beans

This section mulched with plastic to save water and control weeds

Mulched with grass clippings or plastic

Mulched with grass clipping

Mulched with plastic or grass clippings

Close-Row Block Planting
Row Crops
Vine Crops

Size 47' x 20' = 940 Square Feet

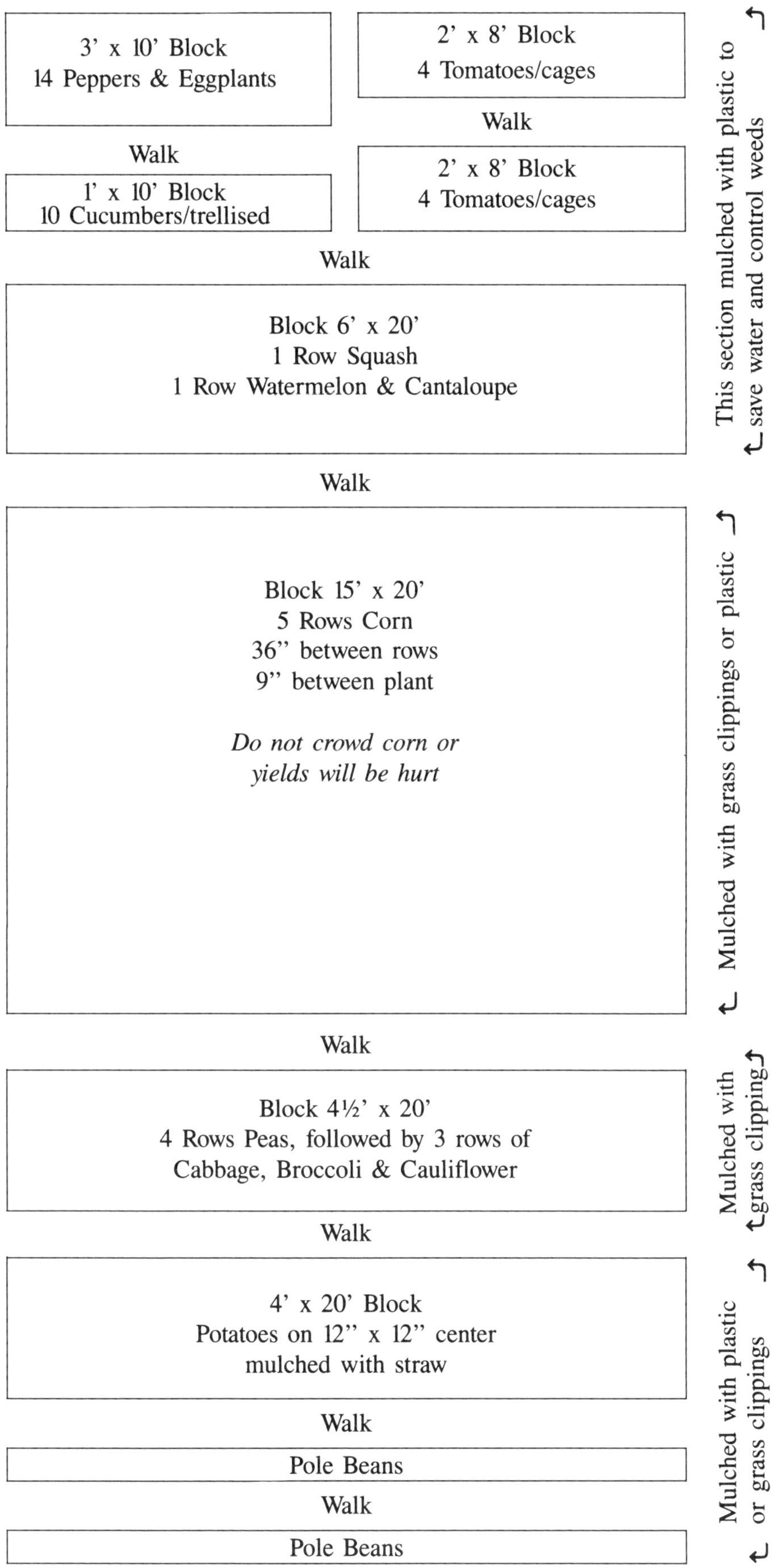

Row and Vine Crops in Traditional Spacing

Garden Size 65' x 20' = 1300 square feet.

3'	Peppers & Eggplant, 13 plants
5'	Tomatoes, 8 plants
5'	Cucumbers, 10 plants
5'	Squash, 8 plants
3'	
3'	
3'	5 Rows Corn
3'	(9" between plants)
3'	
3'	
3'	3 Rows Peas/Fall Cabbage
3'	
3'	
3'	4 Rows Potatoes
3'	
3'	
3'	2 Rows Beans
3'	

65 Feet Long

← 20-Foot Rows →

This same garden can be grown in a close-row block planting for 25% less space.

RAISED BED GARDENING

For centuries, crops in many parts of the world have been produced on modified soils in elevated growing areas between walkways. An archaeological friend tells of evidence of raised bed cropping in ancient America around the time of Christ. Today it still is an excellent approach to maximize vegetable production in a limited space.

Raised beds have the advantage that they help protect the soil from compaction. Walkways or paths are defined, and thus the planting beds are never stepped on. Organic matter can easily be added to improve soil's tilth.

Another big plus with clay soils is that the raised bed will drain faster, allowing for quicker warming and earlier spring plantings. The bed could even be covered with plastic to protect it from spring rains and to speed warming.

Beds can be raised with building materials like lumber or bricks to create a formal planting area. Or, the soil in the typical garden area can be corrugated to make a series of beds and walks.

Try using 2'' by 4'' and 2'' by 6'' lumber for your raised bed boxes. Screw them into a rectangular-shaped frame or edging, set them in place on the garden and add soil and compost. Your objective is to define the walkways from the planting beds. The 4- or 6-inch high boards work well. It makes it easy for children (and their parents) to stay on the outlined walks and off the planting areas. This slight raise is also adequate for drainage from spring rains. You can cover the bed, protecting it from spring storms and allowing for earlier planting. The low box, with the bulk of the rooting zone in the ground, affords some protection from freezing soils for off-season production. Higher boxes could be constructed if there is a need.

Boxes can be designed for special crops. Tomatoes can grow in a box two-feet wide, designed to fit tomato cages. A box width of 36-48 inches is ideal for a kitchen garden (lettuce, spinach, chard, carrots, beets, parsnips, onions, leeks, etc.) You can easily reach from the sides for planting, weeding, and harvesting. Make the length of the box fit the space. In design, remember that you should never need to step in, so you must be able to comfortably reach all areas of the box from the sides.

With fairly good garden soil, just add soil and some compost (or other organic matter). Remove the rocks in the bed area. Gardeners with very poor soils could excavate and re-fill the rooting zone with better soil. (Remember the rooting depths of most vegetables is 2 feet.) If you add a different textured soil, be sure to somewhat mix the two—a line where the different soils merge can interfere with root spread and water movement.

In properly prepared raised beds, the soil remains light and fluffy, it gives maximum utilization in limited space, and it is very suited to close-row block planting systems. Some are sprinkle irrigated, others are drip irrigated. To extend the growing season into the frosty spring and fall, you can easily make a coldframe-type covering with clear plastic on a wire frame.

Raised beds can also be designed without structural sides. This system is fantastic for heavy clay soils.

To construct this system, spread a couple of inches of organic matter over the garden and till it in. It takes 6-7 cubic yards of organic matter to cover 1000 square feet. If you use fresh organic materials, you will need some extra nitrogen to supply the soil bacteria which process this material.

Raised bed garden being constructed by Master Gardener for KSL-TV demonstration use. The beds are raised by digging down the walkways. This corrugated style is great for clay soils. (Photo by David Whiting)

Shape the beds with a shovel or rake, moving soil from the walkway areas up onto the bed areas. A convenient-sized walk is 14-16 inches wide. Make the beds 48-inches wide at their base and 36-inches wide on the top, with the sides tapering in. A convenient height is 8 inches.

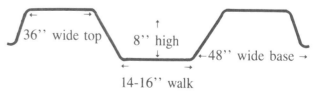

To maintain the bed, keep the entire surface covered with mulch. Grass clippings, compost or sawdust work well. Just pull back the mulch on the top, as needed, to plant. The walks make a great spot to compost the garden refuse. Drop the carrot tops and corn husks in the walk as you harvest. This builds the mulch layer and improves the soil. As needed, more organic materials can be raked from the walks up onto the beds.

Even in heavy clay, the soil will remain relatively soft and will resist compaction. You can replant successive crops without tilling. The established walks absorb the compaction of foot traffic, and the continual mulch protects the seed bed from compaction caused by sprinklers and rain. The beds should be mulched year around and are easily planted the next year without reconstruction.

A friend illustrated another advantage of raised bed gardening. Due to a physical handicap, he has a difficult time getting down to tend his garden without smashing the row behind him. With his raised bed garden (walkways were made a little wider) he could enjoy tending his gardens.

WHEN TO PLANT

The planting times for various vegetables are based on the crops' ability to tolerate cool temperatures and frost, and on the minimum temperatures required for growth. Some crops, like dry onions and peas, are also influenced by the length of the night (photoperiodism).

Average frost dates, length of the growing season and the average summer temperatures dictate what crops can be grown in any given locale.

Spring Planting Time

Spring crops can be planted as soil and air temperatures rise above critical minimums and as the frost period ends. Taking these three factors into account, standard planting times are based on the date of the local average last spring frost.

Gardeners need to understand what is meant by the "date of the average last spring frost." It means there is still a 50-50 chance of a frost after this date. Or, in other words, in 15 of the last 30 years, there has been a frost after this date. It implies no specifics regarding the last frost for any given year.

If you do not know the average last spring frost date for your area, you can get the date from the National Weather Service or from the Cooperative Extension Service office in your county.

Using the average spring frost date as a planting guide has one disadvantage: it does not adjust for warm or cool seasons. Researchers have found that the full bloom on apples coincides with the last average frost date. So, if you live in an apple-growing area, use apple blooming for your planting guide.

Based on temperature needs, vegetables are divided into four planting groups as indicated in the table. Cool wet spring weather may delay the early plantings.

Vegetable Planting Times

Group A, Hardy Vegetables

These vegetables will grow at temperatures as low as 40 degrees and may survive a frosty nip. They prefer cool growing temperatures and loose quality in hot weather. These crops can be planted when the soil dries out in the spring, typically as apple buds swell, about 2-4 weeks before the date of the average last spring frost.

Broccoli	Onions	Radishes
Cabbage	Lettuce	Spinach
Kohlrabi	Peas	Turnips

Group B, Semi-Hardy Vegetables

These vegetables will grow at minimum temperatures of 40-50 degrees but are less tolerant of a frosty night. Cool temperatures will also improve their quality. They are generally planted 2 weeks before the average last spring frost date, as apple buds reach the tight cluster stage.

Beets	Parsley	Swiss Chard
Carrots	Parsnips	
Cauliflower	Potatoes	

Group C, Tender Vegetables

These vegetable require temperatures above 60 degrees, and will not survive a frost. They grow best in the warm summer temperature of 70 to 95 degrees. Plant when apples reach full bloom, around the date of the average last spring frost. (This planting time is based on the assumption that the likelihood of frost will be mostly over before they poke their heads through the soil.)

Dry Beans	Corn
Snap Beans	Cucumbers
Celery	Zealand Spinach
New transplants	Summer Squash

Group D, Very Tender Vegetables

These vegetables require temperature above 60 degrees to grow, and warm summery type weather. Production is limited in cooler mountain valleys. A week of cool temperatures (below 55) will stunt growth, reducing yields. These crops should not be planted until warm weather moves in, about the time little green apples are noticed on the trees, typically 2 weeks after the average spring frost date.

Lima Beans	Pumpkins
Cantaloupes	Winter Squash
Eggplants	Watermelons
Peppers	

Another excellent method to judge planting times for a specific season is based on soil temperatures. This is particularly good on sandy soils which can dry and warm fast. The Germination Temperatures table gives the minimum temperature for various vegetables. Temperature is standardized for measurements taken 4 inches deep, at 8 o'clock in the morning. Experienced gardeners rely heavily on soil temperature as a planting guide; it is an excellent final check for when to plant.

Planting For A Fall Harvest

In the warmer valleys of the Intermountain West, many of the cool-season crops can be summer planted for a fall harvest. If you have not tried a fall garden, you are missing half of the fun. Crops like cabbage, broccoli and cauliflower will be sweeter coming into harvest in the cool fall weather compared to the spring/summer plantings.

These cool-season crops, which do not like the summer heat, will thrive in the 50 and 60 degree temperature of the Intermountain West's beautiful falls. For fall planting dates, figure backwards from the average first fall frost date. Since crop development is slowed in the cooler fall weather, you would do well to add a couple of weeks extra growing time. Example fall planting dates are given below for the Salt Lake City and Logan, Utah areas.

Germination Temperatures Degrees (Fahrenheit)			
Vegetable	Minimum	Optimum	Maximum
Asparagus	50	70	90
Beans	50	80	90
Beets	40	80	90
Broccoli	40	80	90
Cabbage	40	80	90
Cantaloupe	60	90	100
Carrots	40	80	90
Cauliflower	40	80	90
Celery	40	70	80
Chard	40	80	90
Corn	50	80	100
Cucumbers	60	90	100
Lettuce	40	70	70
Okra	60	90	100
Onions	40	80	90
Parsnips	40	70	90
Peas	40	70	80
Peppers	60	80	90
Pumpkins	60	90	100
Radish	40	80	90
Spinach	40	70	70
Squash	60	90	100
Tomatoes	50	80	100
Turnips	40	80	100
Watermelons	60	90	110

Crops for Fall Harvest		
Crop	Planting Time	
	Salt Lake City, Utah	Logan, Utah
Average first fall frost	October 13	October 3
Beets	mid July	early July
Broccoli	early July	late June
Cabbage	early July	late June
Carrots	mid July	early July
Cauliflower	early July	late June
Kohlrabi	late July	mid July
Lettuce, leaf	mid July	early July
Onions, green	mid July	early July
Peas	mid July	early July
Radishes	August	August
Spinach	early August	late July
Swiss Chard	mid July	early July

Growth and Summer Temperatures

As most gardeners understand, crop growth rates are based on summer temperatures. In the warmer valleys, with their longer growing season and higher summer temperatures, gardeners can grow two or three crops of many vegetables. For example, in Salt Lake City, a gardener could grow three non-overlapping harvest periods of corn, while only two such corn plantings are possible in the cooler setting of Logan Utah. It is also interesting to note how the harvest of a crop quickens as the season warms and slows as the season cools off into fall. Compare the various planting/harvest dates for corn in the table. It will suggest your spacing in planting dates.

Harvest Dates as Influenced by Planting Date and Local Temperature			
	Planting Date	Harvest Date	
		Salt Lake City, Utah	Logan, Utah
Corn	May 10	Aug. 10	
80 days to	May 20	Aug. 15	Sept. 2
maturity	May 31	Aug. 21	Sept. 11
	June 10	Aug. 27	Sept. 21
	June 20	Sept. 5	
	June 30	Sept. 16	
	July 10	Oct. 3	
Tomatoes	May 10	July 27	
65 days to	May 20	Aug. 1	Aug. 14
maturity	May 31	Aug. 7	Aug. 20
	June 10	Aug. 13	Aug. 28

SOWING SEEDS

A combination of water, oxygen and heat signals a seed to begin to grow. The water serves to soften the seed coat and to start the chemical processes of growth. Soil should be moist when planting seed. If the soil is dry, run some water down the furrow before seeding.

Over-watering a new seed planting will reduce the oxygen level in the soil and can cause the seed to suffocate. Damping off disease, which rots germinating seeds and seedlings, will be more serious in cold and wet soils. Excessive moisture from heavy rains can likewise interfere with germination.

Before seeding, fertilizer is generally added and cultivated into the soil. Soils are cultivated to fluff up the soil and eliminate crop debris, clods and weeds. The soil surface should be level, light and fluffy; but do not excessively overwork the soil, destroying the soil tilth. Avoid working wet soils; if the soil will form mud balls, it is too wet to cultivate.

Seeds may be planted individually, in hills, or sprinkled down a furrow. A hoe and a hand trowel make good planting tools.

As a rule of thumb, expect 80% of the seeds to germinate and avoid over seeding. Even with small seeds like lettuce and carrots, take a little time to spread the seed evenly. Excessive seed placement is not only wasteful but doubles the work load with its heavy thinning requirements. With proper care, leftover seeds will keep for years.

As a rule of thumb, plant the seed down 3-4 times its diameter. Small seed needs only a very light covering. Fine soil, sand or peat moss can be sprinkled over the tiny seed with a kitchen strainer. On clay soils which crust easily, cover the seed with sand or peat moss.

The seed needs to be kept moist but not water-logged. Spring plantings often do not need additional watering until the crops emerge. A common mistake is to over-water the spring garden. Summer planting may require a light sprinkling once or twice a day to maintain moisture levels.

Be sure to thin the crops when they are very young. Crowding reduces yields and increases disease problems. Crowded radishes will not develop roots. Crowded lettuce will be stronger flavored. Crowded corn develops fewer ears.

STARTING TRANSPLANTS INDOORS

Transplants are a popular way to get a jump on the season. These plants may be started by the gardener or purchased from local nurseries. Many gardeners enjoy starting their own seed. But unless the gardener can provide the proper growing conditions, the transplants will be of poor quality. The factors that must be carefully monitored include soil, temperature, light, fertilization and age of plants at transplanting. These factors must be adjusted to fit the specific needs of the various crops.

Soils

To grow transplants, always use a good soil designed for container use. This soil should hold the needed nutrients and water, but not waterlog readily. For starting seeds, it should be a fine texture. The soil should not contain clay, which packs in a pot like a brick. Gardeners may mix their own growing media or use commercially prepared mixes.

The primary components of potting soils include peat moss, perlite, and vermiculite. Peat moss serves to hold the water and nutrients. Fine-textured peat moss, with its small pore spaces, will easily waterlog. Vermiculite also holds water and nutrients, and the larger particle size will help improve aeration and drainage. Perlite is low in water and nutrient-holding capacity, but is great to increase aeration and soil drainage.

Other forms of organic matter like compost, sawdust, shredded bark, and manures can also be used in potting soils. Their relative properties depend on the materials and their coarseness. Extra nitrogen may be needed to supply the decaying organic matter.

Course sands are used to increase drainage, but may reduce aeration and will increase weight. Calcined clays (kitty litter), which vary considerably in their properties depending on brand, are also used to increase aeration and are low in water and fertilizer-holding ability. Wetting agents, lime (to adjust the pH) and fertilizer are also common components of potting soils.

Packaged "potting soils" are primarily comprised of peat moss or other organic materials, and they will easily hold excessive water. They are readily improved by adding additional perlite or vermiculite. This fluffing agent increases drainage and serves to aerate the soil. Add 1 part of perlite to 3 parts of potting soil. The very fine texture of bagged "seed starting soils" will likewise lend to poor drainage.

Most commercial greenhouse growers rely heavily on *synthetic soils* (also called *soil-less mixes* since they contain no dirt). This potting material is specially formulated for container growing. These mixtures are preferred for commercial production because they are very consistent in their growing properties. They are designed with good water-and nutrient-holding capacities and also drain readily, making water management easy. Synthetic soils come low in nutrients, so the grower has better control over growth rates. Weekly applications of a diluted water-soluble fertilizer is the standard procedure. These soils are basically free of disease organisms. These ready-to-use commercial mixes typically come in 4-cubic-foot bales or 50-pound bags. They are an excellent economical product for home gardeners needing large quantities of soil. We are starting to see these soils available in smaller packages for home gardener use.

Some gardeners prefer to use their own soil. Avoid all soils with clay; these pack too hard for container use. A good garden soil may need amendments of peat moss, perlite or vermiculite to improve its suitability for container use.

Peat pellets are popular with gardeners because they have no soil to spill or mix. Peat moss pellets swell into a planting cube when placed in water. They should be placed in a tray and covered with peat moss to prevent excessive moisture evaporation from their sides. They are suitable only for smaller transplants. Larger plants will outgrow the rooting size.

Containers

In selecting containers for starting plants, consider durability, expense, size and drainage. Undersized rooting areas will stunt upper plant growth. As a rule to thumb, the above-ground portion of the mature transplants should not be more than twice the size of the pot.

Inexpensive plastic pots are available in any shape and size. Today's pots have slightly tapered sides to allow the soil ball to slip out easily without disturbing the roots. The trend by commercial growers is to use square pots which give a large rooting zone for the space used. Most commercial bedding plants and vegetables are grown in pony-pak tray liners which give each plant a growing cell. These are available in many sizes.

Peat pots and peat strips are taking a back seat to the new tapered plastic pots with the newer synthetic soil mixes. Peat pots and strips are fragile and do not tolerate handling. Moisture evaporates through their sides, requiring more care in watering.

Clay pots are somewhat obsolete due to their high cost, weight, and breakability. Clay pots breathe, allowing moisture evaporation from their sides. Excessive moisture-pull from the soil can be reduced by soaking the pots before planting.

Styrofoam growing pots and strips are inexpensive. A lot of the cuttings planted in commercial greenhouses are started and shipped in styrofoam strips. A disadvantage is that the roots tend to stick in the styrofoam, disturbing the root ball as it is removed.

A lot of suitable growing containers are processed through the kitchen each day. Plastic drinking cups, and containers from yogurt, cottage cheese, pop and milk make suitable growing pots with a few drain holes punched in the bottom. Some gardeners try egg cartons, but they are a little small for general use. Basically, any container which will hold the soil, allow for drainage and be stable is suitable.

Seeding

The proper time to start seeds depends on when the plants will be transplanted outside. A common mistake of the home gardener is to start them too early.

The container should be filled to 1/2 inch from the top with lightly moistened soil. A piece of paper towel or newspaper works well to cover drain holes. The soil should be leveled and lightly firm but not packed. Seeds may be placed thinly in shallow furrows or individually planted. The top of a pencil or pen can be used to make nice holes in the soil into which the individual seeds are dropped. As a general rule, a seed should be planted at a depth of 3-4 times its diameter. Seeds can be covered with fine soil, vermiculite or milled peat. Moisten the surface with a fine mist, being careful not to wash the seed out.

Seeding Time for Vegetable Transplants	
Vegetable	Weeks to grow transplant
Asparagus	12 weeks
Celery	10-12 weeks
Cole crops	4-6 weeks
Broccoli, Cabbage	
Cauliflower	
Eggplant	6-8 weeks
Lettuce	3-4 weeks
Onions	8 weeks
Peppers	8 weeks
Tomatoes	6-8 weeks
Vine Crops	2-3 weeks
Cucumbers, Squash,	
Melons	

To keep the moisture in, the container can be covered with a plastic sheet or placed in a plastic bag. Soil heat cables will stimulate germination. Most plants prefer a soil temperature of 65 to 80 degrees.

Plants need bright light as soon as they germinate. Inadequate light is where most home-started transplant projects fail. A coldframe, hot bed or greenhouse is preferred. Gardeners often under-estimate the light in a sunny window. These seedlings require direct sun for the full length of the day. If they receive inadequate light, the plants become tall and spindly.

Artificial light may be used to supplement the growth. Cool white fluorescent tubes are preferred. To provide the high level of light needed for growth, the fluorescent tubes should be lowered to within 2-3 inches of the plants. Supplemental lighting should run 12-14 hours per day and must be turned off at night to give the plants their needed rest. A typical "bright" room is generally not bright enough for plant growth. Standard room lighting will not grow transplants.

Most young transplants prefer daytime temperatures around 65 to 75 degrees. Plants will become spindly or stunted with higher temperatures. Care must be taken that coldframes and greenhouses do not become too hot during the day. Night temperatures should drop 5-10 degrees. The cool season crops (cabbage, cauliflower, broccoli, and lettuce) prefer day temperatures of 60-65 degrees and nights below 55 degrees.

Young seedlings should be kept damp but never water logged. Plants may be gently watered over the top, or watered from the bottom. Allowing the soil to soak up water from the bottom will help control damping off disease. However, never allow the soil to continually soak up water; always pour off the excessive water in the tray. Where bottom watering is not practical, dampening off can be suppressed by adding Captan fungicide to the water. Use one tablespoon of Captan per gallon of water.

The young plants need to grow rapidly at first. Weekly fertilization with a diluted water-soluble fertilizer is desired. This very light but frequent feeding will promote a steady growth rate. Never use a dry granular fertilizer on seedlings; they burn too easily.

As time nears for planting them outdoors, transplants need to be hardened off. This process is to toughen up the tender leaf tissue to tolerate the wild and windy outdoors. Plants can be hardened off by gradually exposing them to the wider temperature variation of the outdoors. Fertilizer and watering may also be held back a little to slow their growth rate. The hardening-off process takes about two weeks.

Cloudy days or evenings are the best time to transplant outdoors. This gives the plants time to adjust to their new home without the pressure of the sun's heat. Where possible, avoid transplanting during the heat of the day. Water the plants after planting with a water-soluble fertilizer (root stimulator). This tells the plants it is time to take off. One to three applications should be made, depending on what other fertilizer has been used. Plants will need to be kept moist for the first couple of weeks, allowing time for their limited root systems to spread.

Young transplants are sensitive to heat, frost, and driving rains, but the most damaging element is wind. Wind dehydrates tender leaves readily. A wind break will be very worthwhile on young plants. Boxes, buckets, boards, sacks, newspapers, milk jugs, tomato cages and leafy tree branches are some ideas of things which can be used.

STORING SEEDS

As part of a family preparedness program, a food storage program should contain a year's supply of garden seeds. When properly stored, seeds can be stored for 2-5 years, depending on kind. In desert climate with its low humidity, stored seeds often last for 5 to 25 years. As a rule of thumb, the small seeds like leeks, onions, and parsnips have the shorter storage life.

Seeds should be kept dry, cool and dark. Low humidity is a must for good seed life. Store them in a moisture proof container. Seeds should be kept in a cool room, basement or cellar. Freezing will not harm them, but repeated freezing and thawing can reduce their life. For maximum life, seeds should be kept in the dark.

Cut your seed bill by purchasing seeds in bulk or in larger packages, often buying enough for 2-3 years at a time. For storage, keep your seeds in a plastic food storage bucket, down in the fruit room with the other food storage items. For easy sorting, similar vegetables are stored together in zip-lock bags. The double container system gives good humidity control.

When there is a question about the viability of seed, it is easy to run a "rag doll" germination test. Place a few seeds on a moist paper towel. Roll the towel up, put it in a plastic bag, and place it in a warm place for a few days. Check the seeds at 3-7 days for germination. If germination is low, the seed can still be used, just seed at a slightly heavier rate, allowing for the seed which will not come up.

6
Extending the Harvest Season with Micro-climate Modification

Gardeners with the interest can add several months to their harvest season by using micro-climate modification techniques. These techniques include the use of hot caps, row covers, cold frames and greenhouses.

The term micro-climate refers to the climatic factors immediately around the plant; temperature is the primary concern. In relation to temperature, there are two primary considerations. The most obvious is frost protection. Another concern, just as important, is the air and soil temperatures desired for plant growth. For example, tomatoes and peppers need summery weather with temperatures from 60 to 90 degrees, while lettuce and spinach prefer the cooler temperatures of 40 to 70 degrees.

With just a little effort, any gardener can add a couple of weeks to both ends of the gardening season. With increased interest and capital, some vegetables can be harvested all 12 months of the year. Factors that must be considered include the minimum night temperature, daytime growing temperature, soil temperature and the hours of sunlight. Some gardeners thrive on the extra growing season, while other gardeners enjoy the winter break.

If you are a gardener interested in off-season production, let your creative ability go and have some gardening fun. With a little understanding of heating principles, you can create the micro-climate needed for crop growth.

Plant coverings made of translucent materials can serve to provide frost protection and enhance daytime growing temperatures. Care must be taken that temperatures do not become too hot under the covering during sunny spring days. At Washington State University, various types of plant coverings were tested, measuring temperatures up to 140 to 180 degrees on sunny spring days. Tender plants which prefer temperatures from 50 to 85 degrees can be stunted or killed by this extra heat. During sunny weather, any type of covering left in place during the day will need an opening to vent out excess heat.

Frost Protection

The natural heat which protects a crop on frosty nights is stored in the soil. A soil which is moist will absorb three times more heat during the day than dry soil will. This can give you 4-6 degrees in frost protection for young plants! Bare soil will absorb four times more heat than a soil covered with grass, weeds or an organic mulch.

Smooth ground, likewise, stores more heat than rough ground. Working with these principles can give you an edge on a frosty night.

Since the heat is stored in the soil, any type of plant covering should be wide and spreading, covering as much ground as is practical. *For frost protection trap the heat from the ground around the plants.* A research team working on frost protection of fruit trees forgot this basic principle and killed their orchard. They covered the trees with large plastic bags, but made the mistake of tying the bags in around the tree trunks. Instead of trapping in the heat from the soil, they excluded the heat.

Gardeners dealing with frost protection should understand the basic differences in the Intermountain West's three types of frosts. The most common type of late spring frost is a *radiation* freeze. It occurs on clear nights when there is no cloud cover to trap in the heat. The coldest part of the night is just before sunrise. These late-spring or early fall radiation frosts typically drop only a few degrees below freezing. Protection is easy with this type of light frost. A simple covering over plants will trap in the heat coming from the soil.

An *advection* freeze is where a cold front brings in cold air. Air temperatures can fall substantially below the freezing point. Storm or cloud cover may reduce the amount of heat collected during the day in the soil.

The most damaging type of spring or fall frost is the combination *radiation-advection* freeze. Here a cold front brings in cold air, and limits heat absorption during the day. What heat is absorbed is readily lost as the sky clears at night.

It takes a little more planning to protect from an advection or advection-radiation freeze. Since heat absorption was reduced during the day, and since temperatures can drop well below freezing, supplemental heat may be necessary. However, gardeners can often get by in the late spring and early fall by doing a little extra planning for their plant covers. The extra factors to account for are wind and rain.

In a rain-frost combination avoid covering materials which will absorb moisture. When a blanket, rug or other water-absorbent material gets wet, there is tremendous evaporative cooling as the wind pulls water vapors from the surface. As water changes from the liquid phase to the vapor phase, heat is pulled from the surrounding area.

Temperatures under a wet blanket can be several degrees colder than the general air temperature. The evaporative cooling effect is minimized with waterproof materials. Wind complicates these situations by blowing covers off, by pulling warm air out, and by enhancing evaporative cooling.

People often get concerned about a light snow falling on their tender garden or flowers. Snow is not a problem; it is the temperature at the plant that is critical.

Another consideration that must be mentioned related to frost covers is conductive heat transfer. Where a plastic type covering touches a plant, heat will be conducted from the warmer plant to the plastic. Plants can freeze where they touch the plastic. Plastic coverings should be held up off the plants.

Using Sprinklers for Frost Protection

When a late spring frost threatens the young garden, sprinklers can provide some frost protection. This technique is widely used in commercial strawberry and vegetable fields of the southwest. You can use it to protect your garden plantings and bedding plants. However, it is not practical for fruit trees because the weight of the ice can break down the tree.

Basically, the irrigation sprinklers are turned on when temperatures dip to freezing. As water freezes it releases large quantities of energy. This heat release can keep the crop from freezing. Do not turn on the water until the temperatures reach near freezing, typically around 4:00 to 5:00 in the morning. Running the water all night will overwater the cool soil! Do not turn off the sprinklers until all the ice has melted. Turning off the sprinklers when the temperature rises above freezing, but with ice on the plants, can lead to frost injury.

Hot Caps

A covering over an individual plant is called a hot cap. It could be placed over the plant for the early growing season or simply set out to cover it on a cold night. Hot caps could be the standard hat of newspaper or waxpaper, or the popular plastic milk jug. When anticipating a frosty night, gather up the kids' sand buckets, the mop buckets, and empty plant pots to cover crops for the night. Whatever you use as hot caps, take care that the plants do not become too hot during the day. Any covering left on in sunny weather will need a opening to vent out excess heat.

Several types of specially designed hot caps are commercially available. The most talked about is the "Wall of Water." It is a ring of plastic tubes you fill with water. The ring sets around the plant, shielding it from wind and cold. The top is open to allowing for heat escape and plant growth. Inside, night temperatures are warmed from heat absorbed by the water during the day. But the ingenious concept in the wall of water is a simple application of a physics principle. When water freezes, it releases a significant amount of heat. This heat release can protect a plant down to temperatures in the mid teens.

The "Wall of Water" holds three gallons of water, making it wind resistant. It has even protected plants in 100+ mile-per-hour east canyon winds. The Walls of Water froze, but the plants were fine inside. The only problem some gardeners have had with them is children knocking them down.

A Wall of Water solar hotcap protects tomatoes for extra early production. The soil is warmed with a plastic mulch to trap in heat. To promote early growth in the cool spring, use a water-soluble fertilizer with ammonium nitrate as the nitrogen base. (Photo by David Whiting)

Early peppers are protected and warmed under a plastic tent-like row covering. Water-filled milk jugs close to the plant provide heat for the colder nights. (Heat is released as the water freezes.) A plastic mulch traps in heat to warm the soil for early root growth. Temperatures dropped to 12 degrees, but this system protected the peppers! (Photo by David Whiting)

Row Coverings

You can cover your vegetables in their beds with clear plastic on a frame of concrete-reinforcing mesh. Similar fencing materials could be used. It makes an arch over the bed to trap the heat. Clothes pins hold the plastic in place. The plastic can be easily rolled up on warm days. On sunny windy days, you can partially roll down the plastic, leaving some as a wind protection for tender plants. This type of covering will give several degrees of added protection. You can gain 2-4 weeks on both sides of the growing season with this instant cold frame-type covering.

In recent years, several specially designed fabrics have come on the market for frost protection coverings. The most popular is "Reemay." It is great but rather expensive. This light weight, porous fabric can be used with or without support, and can be used to screen out insects. Numerous types of hoop and wire frames are commercially available for row coverings.

You can use the same wire frames to hold a 25-50% shade cloth in the summer to cool crops from the summer heat.

Plastic cold frame row covering over the vegetable bed is constructed of 4 mil plastic held on a frame of concrete-reinforcing mesh. Clothes pins hold the plastic on. (Photo by David Whiting)

Cold frame row covering partially opened for sunny days. This partial covering protects the crop from cool winds. (Photo by David Whiting)

Cold Frames and Hotbeds

By definition, cold frames and hotbeds are miniature greenhouses, or a greenhouse too small for a person to walk inside. A cold frame refers to a structure without a heat source. A hotbed is a heated cold frame. They can be constructed with a minimal cost.

Pictured on page 50 is a plan for a standard wood-sided cold frame. The author built one for early vegetable production from lumber salvaged from a construction site and a large wood frame window screen. The screen material was replaced with an inside and outside layer of 4-mil clear plastic. His only expense was the purchase of two hinges to hold the window screen on as a lid.

In this simple cold frame, the author seeded cool-season crops like lettuce, spinach, radishes and chard four weeks ahead of normal plantings. The cold frame went through 100-mile-per-hour freezing east canyon winds, and only the outside east row had damage. Now he widely uses wire/plastic archs over the beds to achieve the same results. This type of covering will protect plants through a radiant frost and a mild advective frost.

Solar Heated Cold Frames

Gardeners with interest in off-season production will enjoy a solar heated cold frame. With tight construction, good solar principles and insulation, a passive solar-heated cold frame is capable of growing cool-season vegetables through the winter without much supplemental heat.

In the fall of 1989, the author and a friend designed and constructed a passive *Solar Cold frame.* It was designed for off-season vegetable production and for starting transplants. They hoped to gain a couple of months on both ends of the growing season. The result during the winter of 89-90 was impressive. Inside temperatures remained above freezing throughout the winter! The cold frame is 4 feet by 8 feet and stands 4 feet tall on the north wall. It is oriented from east to west, with a glazed south- facing sloped wall.

Basic to a solar cold frame design are some principles of heating and heat loss. Cold air infiltration is the quickest way to cancel out the heating ability of a structure. Special attention should be taken in design and construction to reduce the chances of air infiltration. Exposed joints should

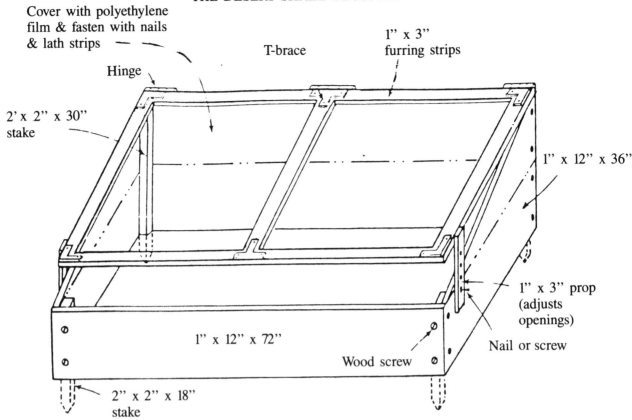

Cover with polyethylene film & fasten with nails & lath strips

Hinge

T-brace

1" x 3" furring strips

2' x 2" x 30" stake

1" x 12" x 36"

1" x 3" prop (adjusts openings)

1" x 12" x 72"

Wood screw

Nail or screw

2" x 2" x 18" stake

Standard Cold Frame for Extending the Growing Season

be thoroughly caulked. Since frost action on a wooden foundation can quickly knock the frame out of kilter, a cement or cement block foundation is desirable.

As they started building the structure, they had some large, heavy, hard-wood pallets on hand. They built the main box structure from these pallets set on their sides. The structure was buried two feet into the ground to provide an insulated rooting area and to anchor the structure from extreme east-canyon winds. The heavy 2" by 6" lumber of the pallets made a nice strong foundation. While the box is not air tight, it screwed together into a very solid frame.

Being aware that wind sucks the warm air out of a structure, they next circled the pallet box with heavy plastic. A layer of 3/4-inch foil-coated urethane foam insulation came next. The insulation covers the north, east and west walls. To keep the rooting zone warm, the underground box area was also covered on the sides and bottom with insulation. The above-ground insulation was covered with 1/4-inch outdoor plywood to protect the insulation from sunlight and mechanical damage.

An alternative wall system, suggested by the experts at Rodale Press, calls for a 2" by 4" frame structure. Walls are constructed with 1/4-inch plywood on both the inside and outside. Walls are insulated to an R value of 12.5 with a 1" and a 1 1/2" sheet of Styrofoam. Avoid fiberglass-

and cellulose-type insulations which will be damaged from moisture accumulation inside the walls.

For glazing they acquired two scraps of Polygal, a rigid double-wall greenhouse covering material. This particular material is difficult to locate in local markets and runs $4-5 per square foot. Their scraps were salvaged pieces cut off a commercial greenhouse construction project.

Other excellent glazing materials include the rigid lexan greenhouse plastic and Plexiglas. Greenhouse-grade fiberglass is less expensive but will have a greater heat loss. Polyethylene plastic is not recommended for the outer glazing. It is ineffective in trapping the long wave, heat-producing radiation.

For year-round use, double glazing which creates an insulating dead-air space is a must for a cold frame. Polyethylene plastic is suitable for the inner layer.

The cold frame door should be small. The large glazed lids of a traditional cold frame easily warps, allowing for cold air infiltration. A small door also lets in less cold air when opened.

Not having the carpenter's tools to make strong frames to hold the glazing materials as doors, they constructed some simple slide tracks out of plywood. The glazing slides in place. It has proven to be very wind tight and easy to open and close as needed.

Solar cold frame built from wood pallets turned on their side. The structure is buried two feet into the ground to provide an insulated rooting space and protection from winds. Plastic circles the wood to seal the box from cold-air infiltration. (Photo by Steve Jenkins)

The solar cold frame box was insulated above and below ground with a layer of foil-coated urethane foam insulation. The below-ground insulation was necessary to keep the root zone warm for winter production. (Photo by Steve Jenkins)

The completed solar cold frame with a 1/4-inch plywood outer wall in place and painted. The south-facing glazing is of double wall, rigid Polygal greenhouse plastic. It slides in a wood track to open. Note the 45-degree angle of the south glazing designed to intercept maximum sunlight in the spring. The tall back (north) wall provides storage space for a solar collector. The east and west walls are insulated. (Photo by David Whiting)

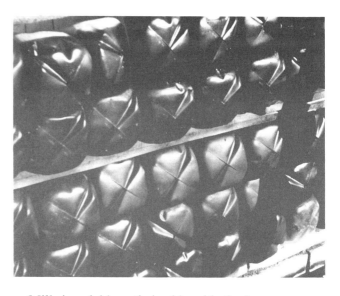

Milk jugs laid on their side with the bottoms out make an excellent solar collector. Jugs are painted black to maximize energy collection. (Photo by David Whiting)

The south-facing glazed wall is cut to a 45-degree angle. This angle was selected to maximize the sun input in March. The sun is at an approximate 45-degree angle with the earth at this time of year in northern Utah. This angle also gives a large glazed surface to intercept more sunlight. The tall back wall created by the angle provided area for the solar heat collectors.

To store the sun's heat the back wall is stacked brick-like with water-filled milk jugs. These jugs absorb up to 90 percent of the sun's energy. A pinch of clorox is added to the water to prevent algae growth. Without the clorox, the warm-water jugs will turn to a slimy green soup. The lids are secured on with a ring of caulking inside the cap.

To provide a good surface for sun interception, the jugs are laid on their sides, with the bottoms showing. They are sprayed with a flat black paint to maximize solar absorption. This 4' x 8' x 4' cold frame held 112 jugs. A shelf is needed for each two rows of jugs.

To reflect sunlight back onto the plants, the interior was painted glossy white. The underground portions were painted with Green #10 wood preserver. The outside surfaces were painted to tie in with the yard landscaping. Other expenses in the project included a roll of insulating tape to seal around the glazing and a tube of caulking to seal the seams in the plywood.

They did not install an insulative night curtain. (Solar design calls for a movable insulative panel to shield the glazed areas at night.) When placed in the interior of the structure, a night curtain blocks the solar collector when opened. In the event of forecasted extreme low temperatures, they can place an aluminum space blanket over the glazing to reflect back the stored heat. If additional heat is desired, a soil heat cable would be an economical heating method.

During the winter of 89-90, the solar-heated milk jug cold frame performed better than anticipated. Day-time temperatures were maintained nicely for cool season vegetables. Outside night temperatures dropped during a winter storm with heavy winds to zero, but inside temperatures remained above freezing.

Like any solar-heated unit, the critical point is when prolonged periods of cloud cover are accompanied by a sub-zero artic express-type freeze. Under these conditions when solar input is minimized, a supplemental heat source may be necessary to protect crops from freezing.

In this cold frame they have successfully grown cool-season vegetables during the winter. Lettuce and spinach were planted on New Years Day. With the short day length this time of year, growth rates are slower. Plants grow on clear sunny days but stand still on stormy or smoggy days. The lettuce was ready to start harvesting the first part of February, the spinach was a little slower. January 1 is not the recommended planting time for lettuce, but it was impressive to see how well it grew.

Spinach and lettuce in solar cold frame in mid-February. Temperatures dropped below zero but the temperature was maintained superbly through the winter for these cool-season crops. (Photo by David Whiting)

The concept of solar-heated cold frames or greenhouses as a season extender merits serious consideration by the gardener inclined to year-round activities. In mountain valleys with their clear sunny winter days, there is a winter gardening season for cool season crops.

Solar Greenhouse for Off-season Production

The same principles which apply to the solar-heated cold frame would transfer to a solar greenhouse. A greenhouse is basically a cold frame large enough to walk inside. A solar greenhouse must be well insulated, wind tight, with an efficient solar collector.

In the Utah State University's Solar Greenhouse Complex in Farmington, Utah, vegetable crops are harvested through the winter. Beautiful cool-season vegetables grow through the winter in these passive solar units without supplemental heat. Outside temperatures dropped to the minus teens without freezing crops. Crop growth, however, was non-existent during a January with 29 days of smog and fog.

As a point of clarification, it is not cost effective to grow vegetables in a traditionally heated greenhouse during the cold winter months of the Intermountain West. Winter vegetable production cannot be justified solely on economics, even in a solar greenhouse. While a solar greenhouse is less expensive to heat, it is more expensive to construct. It is not cost effective to grow vegetables for harvest under artificial lights. Those who garden for relaxation and pleasure may find a solar structure worthwhile.

Guidelines for Off-season Vegetable Production

Vegetables do not grow as automatically during the spring, winter and fall, as in the summer. Special care must be given to growing temperatures, water and fertilizer. Temperatures fluctuate widely in any growing structure. The lack of temperature control is the number one problem with off-season growing. Keep a thermometer handy to give you a guide on how you're doing. Soil temperatures arc often a limiting factor for early spring plantings in a growing structure.

With the cool soil temperatures associated with off-season production, use a water-soluble balanced fertilizer with ammonium nitrate as the nitrogen source. Nutrients in this type of fertilizer are readily usable by the plant. As a general rule, fertilize weekly with this mild fertilizer solution.

Plants must be kept moist, but take extra care not to over-water them. The cooler soils will be slow to dry when over-watered. Select good garden or potting soils which are high in organic matter and coarse enough to drain readily.

Cool-season vegetables do well in a solar cold frame or solar greenhouse. High temperatures are not needed, and an occasional dip to freezing will not harm the crops. High light intensity is not as critical as with warm-season vegetables.

Winter vegetables should be planted in the fall so that the crop is nearing maturity by mid October. During the winter months, the short day length and lower light intensity will significantly reduce crop growth. However, the biggest factor influencing crop growth is winter storms. When there are several days of heavy cloud cover or temperature inversions which result in smog, crop growth comes to a halt. The crops sit in limbo without the sun.

Cool-season crops prefer a daytime temperature of 50 to 70 degrees. The night-time temperature will drop slightly, generally from 45 to 55 degrees. These crops will tolerate any short-term temperature extreme ranging from freezing to 90 degrees.

Cool-season crops to consider in a solar cold frame or greenhouse include the following:

BEETS are easy to grow off-season if properly thinned. Root growth may be reduced in mid-winter, but young beets for greens do well.

COLE CROPS (Cabbage, Broccoli, Cauliflower, Brussel Sprouts, Kohlrabi) are frost tolerant and may be grown without much supplemental heat. Avoid long-term temperature extremes which lead to bolting (rapid flower head formation). You'll probably have good success with broccoli, fair luck with cauliflower, and ok success with cabbage. The kolhrabi will be fantastic. For cabbage, cauliflower and broccoli, consider a minimum root-zone size of 10-inches deep and 5 gallons of soil per plant.

CARROTS can be extremely sweet if grown with adequate water and cool temperatures. Since carrots can be grown in the garden and stored in the ground through the winter, the space will be better used by other crops.

CHARD does extremely well in off-season production. It is more tolerant of the temperature fluctuations common to cold frames or greenhouses. Is is one of the best crops for winter growing.

LETTUCE is the number-one candidate for year round production. Select from the soft head or leaf types. The cool temperature of winter will produce tender, sweet lettuce. Strong flavors result from overcrowding, water stress and hot temperatures. Lettuce prefers a daytime temperature of 60 degrees, with nighttime temperatures around 45-50 degrees. Try to keep the temperatures under 70 degrees for best quality.

Mid-winter lettuce production in a solar greenhouse. (Photo by David Whiting)

GREEN ONIONS, the bunching onions or scallion, do well with adequate watering. The common bulb-type dry onion is sensitive to the length of the day and is not suitable for winter production.

PEAS are not normally grown in a cold frame or greenhouse; their yield is low for the space required. But if you like fresh edible pod or sugar peas for salads or stir fry, they will grow. Temperature extremes will cut pod development. Powdery Mildew may be a problem in the higher humidity.

RADISHES are a good choice for fall and spring production. They are not suitable for winter growth, because they require 12 hours of sun per day to develop the root. Ideal temperatures are 60 to 72 degrees for daytime and 55 at night. Avoid water stress and high temperatures which lead to hot roots.

SPINACH does only fair in winter production. Growth rates are rather slow in the low-light periods. It does not like temperature fluctuations and prefers a cool temperature around 45-50 degrees.

The warm-season vegetables are much more demanding in off-season production. They require high light intensity and moderate night temperatures. Production is poor in cloudy or smoggy weather. Accurate temperature control is essential for fruit set, and hand pollination is required on many crops.

Warm-season vegetables need a daytime temperature from 60 to 85 degrees. Night temperatures should be maintained at 55 to 60 degrees. Short-term temperature extremes range from 50 to 100 degrees. Due to the higher temperature required for production of these crops, it is unlikely that a passive solar greenhouse will supply adequate warmth without additional heat during the stormy periods.

Warm-season crops which will grow off season in a solar cold frame or greenhouse include the following:

CUCUMBERS are semi-tropical and thus adaptive to greenhouse production. They are very demanding in greenhouse management. To grow tender, sweet cucumbers, they must have a warm location with high light intensity, high humidity and good moisture. Try planting them in a barrel with a trellis. Minimum rooting space is 8 inches deep, and 2 gallons of soil per plant is needed. Select from the gynoecious (female flowers only) or greenhouse varieties.

Temperature control is critical. Daytime temperatures should be 75 to 80 degrees, and 5-10 degrees cooler on cloudy days. Nighttime temperatures must be maintained above 50 degrees. Off-flavored cucumbers will develop if the temperature fluctuates more than 20 degrees. Most hobby growers do not manage their greenhouse this closely.

VINE CROPS, SQUASH, CANTALOUPES AND WATERMELONS are not generally grown in the greenhouse simply because they use too much space. But they can be. They require high light intensity and a daytime temperature of around 80 degrees. They have male and female flowers and will require hand pollinations. Trellising will conserve space. Vine crops will need a minimum of 5 gallons of soil per plant. Watch for powdery mildew which is common in the higher humidity of the greenhouse.

TOMATOES AND PEPPERS are the most popular greenhouse crops of the warm-season vegetables. During the day, they need high light intensity and temperature between 70 and 80 degrees. Nights should drop to 60-70 degrees. Temperatures below 55 degrees or above 90 degrees will interfere with fruit set. They will require hand pollination. Minimum soil needs for peppers is 2 gallons of soil per plant, at least 8-inches deep. Tomatoes need 5 gallons of soil per plant, at least 12-inches deep, except for the small vine patio types.

Mid-winter bean production in a solar greenhouse. (Photo by David Whiting)

7
Growing Vegetables

Growing superior-quality garden vegetables comes from the gardener's ability to meet the specific growing needs of each crop. Some crops like it hot, others like it cold. Many crops will become strong if the soil becomes slightly dry. Yields are often influenced by spacing and by weather.

This chapter indicates the general growing needs of each vegetable. Similar crops and vegetable families have been grouped for discussion. Where special attention is needed to maximize quality and yields, those special needs have been indicated. Some of the newer research findings will change many of the old standard growing practices. Watch for the hints and grow your best garden ever!

ASPARAGUS

The key to asparagus production is good fertilization. At least twice a year, sprinkle nitrogen fertilizer on and water it in. The first application should be applied in the spring as growth starts. Make a second application at the end of the harvest season.

Another factor in generating heavy production is to avoid over harvesting. The strength of the root system will determine the productivity of the patch the following spring. When the spears start to decrease in size, cease harvesting. This channels the plant growth into feeding the roots. The fern of the asparagus plant should never be removed until fall frost time. Again, this leafy surface is needed to strengthen the roots. Asparagus has male and female plants. The female plants will produce red berries on their ferns.

Asparagus does not compete well with other plants nor with weeds. Weeds can be controlled with organic mulches. Do not skimp on water during production time.

Asparagus likes a soil rich in organic matter. A little extra work in preparing the planting bed will pay off over the years of production. The bed area should be dug 12 inches deep with 4 inches of decomposed organic matter (compost, peat moss, manure, etc.) mixed with the soil.

Asparagus can be direct seeded or started from roots. Using roots is more expensive, but the bed will be ready for its first harvest in just two years compared to three years.

When planting roots, start by soaking them in warm water for a couple of hours. This softens up the roots for planting. Dig a trench 12 inches wide and 4 to 5 inches deep. Spread the roots out like arms of an octopus, 12-18" apart in the trench, and cover them with only two inches of soil. As the shoots grow up, the remaining soil can be added. Some texts suggest planting depths of 6-10 inches. The U.S.D.A. found lower yields with this deeper planting. In colder areas, a winter mulch will help protect the roots with this shallower planting.

Rutgers University, New Jersey, reports that seed-started asparagus can be ready for its first harvest in two years if started indoors and transplanted out. Start the seeds 12 weeks before transplanting, and plant them in a trench as described above, after frosts. These young seedlings for transplanting must be grown in a warm sunny location.

No harvesting should be done the first year, and only limited harvesting the second season. The roots need to become well established and producing stocky spears before serious harvesting begins.

Harvest the spears when they reach 6-8 inches. A good patch may need harvesting every 1-3 days. Cut the spears off with a knife at an angle, just under the soil line. They can also be harvested by snapping. This prevents damaging the unseen spears about to poke through the surface. The spear tips are the most tender portion. Be careful not to over-cook this delicate vegetable.

Standard varieties of heavy production include "Mary Washington" and "Waltham Washington."

BEANS

The bean family represents a large collection of assorted types from all over the world. The common garden "snap" bean is the second-most-popular vegetable grown by home gardeners. The term "string" bean comes from the old varieties of snap beans which had fibrous strings along the pod seam. The string was removed as the beans were snapped. Plant breeders eliminated the strings more than a half a century ago, but the name is still around.

Other common beans include lima beans, edible soy beans, mung beans, dry beans (pintos, great northern, navy, kidney, white), cowpeas (black-eyed peas) and the romano Italian bean. The garbanzo bean or chick pea is not a bean but a legume, related to clover. Each ethnic culture has its type of bean considered to be the best.

Snap Beans

Snap beans are either pole type or bush type. The bush types are most popular, not requiring trellising and training. Pole beans take a little longer to come into production and have the reputation of being heavier producers over a longer season. However, the newer "Blue Lake" bush types sometimes out-produce the poles, also producing until frost.

The dry climate of the Intermountain West is ideal for growing beans, making the Snake River Valley of Idaho the center of world bean seed production. Research from the University of Idaho provides several hints for improving bean yields.

Do not rush the spring planting of beans. University of Idaho researchers found a significant yield reduction when soil temperature dropped below 50 degrees! Or in other words, the soil temperature needs to consistently stay above 50, as measured at 6-inches deep, at 8:00 in the morning. This research suggests that gardeners often rush the planting time in cool seasons; soils typically reach this temperature in mid- to late-May in the warmer valleys.

Plant spacing is another highly researched variable influencing yield. Research from the University of Idaho suggests spacings of 24" (or greater) between rows with 2" between plants, or 18" between rows with 3" between plants, or 12" between rows with 4" between plants, or the equal distant spacing of 6" between rows with 6" between plants. Their work found a 20% increase in yields with the 12" row spacing compared to the 24" row spacing. For maximum production use the 12" by 4" or the 6" by 6" spacing. Overcrowding will not increase yields but will increase disease problems.

Irrigation is critical for successful bean production. Good moisture is required for bean germinations, and irrigation is needed before planting beans in dry soils. However, bean seed is very prone to rotting in cool wet soils.

During blooming and pod production, beans have the highest water use of all vegetables. Any water stress will cause bean blossoms to drop. Likewise, any water standing in the rows at blossom time can be harmful. Pollywog-shaped pods are also a sign of water stress. Pollywogging is where the top of the bean pod fills out but the bottom does not.

In 1989, many gardeners complained of poor bean production; this was caused from water stress induced by the unusually heavy amount of drying south winds. In many gardens the plants would just recover from this extra-heavy water need, and then another round of wind would drop the blossoms again.

Blossom drop can also be induced by temperatures above 97 degrees. Bean diseases which interfere with the movement of water through the roots and stems will also slow or stop production.

Beans are low users of nitrogen, and heavy nitrogen fertilization will lead to excessive vine growth. This does not mean that they do not need some fertilizer. High yields are dependent upon good early vine growth. A light nitrogen application should be made at planting or early in the season.

Beans are extremely sensitive to salty soils. Salt problems show as spotty germination and stunted growth. Leaf margins can burn from the concentration of salt in the leaf. When an overall good garden has a poor bean stand, salt problems should be suspected. In home gardens, salt problems can develop from the overuse of potassium fertilizers.

Snap beans should continue to produce until fall frost takes out the patch. Factors which may prevent this would include water stress, disease, insect problems, lack of harvesting and poor varieties. The Blue Lake types, available as bush or pole, are particularly noted for season-long production.

For tender sweet beans, harvest them as they reach the diameter of a pencil. This will require picking a couple of times a week. Harvesting at this young stage also keeps the plants in prime production. Allowing pods to over size will slow or stop blooming.

Blue Lake Bush or Pole type beans are considered tops in flavor, tenderness and yield. The bush variety "Blue Lake Bush #274" is an amazingly heavy producer. The yellow or wax bean, like "Goldcrop," can add some variety to the table.

Lima Beans

Lima Beans have the same growing practices as snap beans. They require hotter weather, full sun, and are planted at the onset of summer weather. Lima beans are a little larger than snap beans and will need a little extra room.

For best quality harvest lima beans as soon the pod bulges and you can feel the beans. Lima beans are shelled out much like peas, with the pod opening easily if they are mature. "Fordhook" and "Kingston" are popular varieties.

Dry Beans

While most gardeners do not grow dry beans, they are inexpensive to purchase and do very well in the home garden. The most popular varieties include Great Northern, Pinto, Navy and Red Kidney beans.

Dry beans have the same cultural practices as snap beans. They will need a reduction in summer irrigations from mid-August to the early September harvest. Water use cuts sharply as the pods dry down.

Allow the pods to dry and turn brittle before harvesting. Shell out the bean seeds and spread them out to dry. Store them in a rodent-proof container.

Beets - see Root Crops

Cantaloupes - see Vine Crops

Carrots - see Root Crops

Celery - see Leafy and Salad Vegetables

Chard - see Leafy Vegetables

COLE CROPS

Cole crops thrive in cool temperatures; 65-80 degrees is preferred. Established plants will tolerate a frost down to the lower 20's. Hot weather will greatly reduce the sweetness.

Cole crops can be direct seeded or set out as transplants. Space the plants 18-inches apart. Spring plantings are best as transplants. While the plants like cool weather, the seeds do not like cold soils. Start transplants 4-6 weeks before setting them out. Hardened-off transplants can go out 2-4 weeks before the average frost date.

Spring plantings have a disadvantage in the warmer valleys of the Intermountain West; cole crops will come into heading during the summer heat. This reduces their sweetness, makes the harvest period short, and can cause bolting (rapid flower formation making the plant useless).

Premium Crop Broccoli provides excellent quality, with large heads. (Photo by David Whiting)

Planting for a fall harvest is preferred for superior quality and ease of winter storage. Along Utah's Wasatch front, with its average frost date of mid-October, you can direct-seed the crop the first of July. Adjust the time accordingly for your local frost dates. Crops will be ready about frost time and can go directly into pit storage for winter use.

Cole crops are heavy feeders. Any stress from lack of feed or water will decrease their quality. Sandy soils should be supplemented with organic matter to hold the water and nutrients needed. They will need routine control for cabbage worms and occasional aphid problems (see the insect section).

Broccoli

The edible part of broccoli is the immature flower head. If allowed to over-mature even a few days during warm weather, the flowers will open, making the head useless. Side-shoots will develop after the main head is harvested. These shoots are small in comparison, but add to the total yield. The broccoli variety "Premium Crop" stands superior.

Small side shoots will develop on Broccoli after the main head is harvested.

Brussel sprouts grow as little cabbages up the main stem of the plant. (Photos by David Whiting)

The crinkly leaves of the "Savoy Ace Cabbage" are sweeter than the European types. Cole crops are best when grown for harvest during the cool fall weather. (Photo by David Whiting)

Brussels Sprouts

This is an interesting plant to grow. The small cabbages or sprouts develop up the stem, starting from the bottom. Remove the lower leaves as needed to make room for the sprouts. Pinching out the top of the plant when it reaches 20 inches will speed the production, but reduce yields. Harvest the sprouts as they reach ping pong ball size.

Cabbage

Cabbage can be harvested as soon as the head size reachs a soft ball stage. If summer production is coming too fast, you can extend the harvest season by giving the head a 1/2 turn twist. This breaks some of the roots and slows growth. Cabbage is a biennial, flowering its second season. But 2-3 weeks of temperatures below 50 degrees will cause cabbage to bolt (flower early) and the crop is useless. Warm weather will cause the heads to split.

There are many good cabbage varieties. Many gardeners prefer "Savoy Ace." This domestic-type cabbage has a sweeter sap then the European and Danish types. Other popular varieties include "Market Prize" and "Ruby Ball."

Cauliflower

This vegetable is a little more fussy about cold temperatures. It is generally not planted until two weeks before the last spring frost date. Like broccoli, the immature flower head is eaten. To blanch the head (keep it snowy white), tie up the center leaves with an elastic band as the head begins to form.

Cauliflower does not head well in hot weather. For easy production, plant it for harvest in the cool weather of September. The leaves are tied up with an elastic to blanch the cauliflower head white. (Photos by David Whiting)

Kohlrabi

This vegetable adds an interesting crunch to salads and can be cooked like a turnip. The spaceship-looking plant tastes like a cross between turnips and cabbage. The edible portion is the round ball-like stem which develops just above the soil line. Harvest it when the stems widen to two inches. It will become tough and fibrous if allowed to grow large. Kohlrabi is direct seeded. Space the plants about nine inches apart.

CORN

The hints for a superior crop of corn are to watch for the newer sweeter varieties, and to give it lots of space, water and fertilizer. The first planting can be made as apples reach full bloom, at the time of the last average spring frost.

Being a member of the grass family, corn loves nitrogen fertilizer. Side-dress it (apply nitrogen fertilizers during the growing season) every three weeks to maintain a deep rich green color. Remember to keep the application light: one cup of 21-0-0 per 50-foot row works nicely. Evenly sprinkle the fertilizer on the soil before irrigation and let the water wash it in. Fertilization and good water will increase the plants' height and yield.

Corn is also a heavy water user, particularly during silking. A pre-plant irrigation will be needed in dry soils. Since corn does not like wet feet, be careful not to waterlog it during early growth. Water use peaks as the plants tassel and silk. Any water shortage at this time will interfere with pollination, causing the ears to have gaps. During this critical time, be aware of drying winds which increase the water demand.

Since corn is one of America's leading crops, corn growing is a highly researched topic. Many gardeners are unaware of the correct spacings. Corn has a type of metabolism which necessitates maximum sunlight. Overcrowding or planting it in hills will reduce the sun's input on the leaves, significantly cutting the yields. Extreme overcrowding can eliminate ear production. If the rows are 36 inches apart, the corn should be thinned to 9 inches between single plants. If the rows are 30-inches apart, thin to 12 inches between single plants. With this spacing, you will get 3-7 ears per plant on many popular varieties. With proper spacing, some varieties will tiller readily, that is send up side shoots from the base. These side shoots should be left to develop, increasing the yield potential.

Corn is wind pollinated and needs to be planted in blocks. Pollen falls from the tassels (male flowers) to the silks (female flowers). When it is planted in a single row, the pollen shower is too sparse. Blocks should be at least 3 rows wide, but 4-5 rows are preferred to give the block a heavier pollen shower. Inadequate pollination shows as skipped kernels on the ear. Bees also actively gather the pollen. Rows need not be long. For example, a block with 20-foot rows could have the first 10 feet planted for the first crop, with a 5 foot middle section planted for a second crop, and the last 5 foot section planted for a third crop.

In the Intermountain West's warm mountain valleys, two or three crops can be planted for a continual harvest through the summer and fall. Since crop development is based on temperature, planting at two-week intervals will not necessarily put the crops two weeks apart at harvest.

A good rule of thumb for continuous harvest is to plant the next crop when the previous batch of corn plants has 3-4 leaves and is about 6 inches tall.

Corn is wind pollinated and must be planted in blocks, but bees also actively gather corn pollen. When using insecticides, care must be taken to protect these pollinating insect friends. (Photo by David Whiting)

Corn is ready for harvest about three weeks after silking. Silks will dry, the husks will feel tight, and the kernels have a milky juice. Some gardeners check by opening the tip of the cob, but this can open the ear up to insect visitors.

In recent years, plant breeders have developed two new types of corn with higher sugar content. The Sugar Extender gene-type corns have a higher sugar content than standard varieties. Conversion of sugars to starch is also slowed. Sugar Extender-type corns are described as creamy in texture, with a tender gourmet flavor. Isolation from other types of corn is suggested but not required. Popular Sugar Extender-types of corn include "Kandy Corn," "Miracle," "Platinum Lady" and "Double Delight."

The "Super Sweet" gene types have two to three times the sugar content of standard varieties. They hold better for shipment and have a longer harvest period. Even after the ears begin to look old (four weeks after the harvest of the first ears off the patch) they are still sweeter than the standard varieties. Super Sweet corn must be isolated from other non-super sweet types, for any cross pollination will result in a starchy, tough product. Super Sweet varieties require warmer soils for germination, so do not rush their planting in cool wet springs. Popular Super Sweet corns include "Early Extra Sweet," "Landmark" and "Super Sweet Jubilee."

The most popular standard-type corn is "Golden Jubilee."

Isolation of the three types (super sweet, sugar enhancer and standard gene types) is defined as 300 feet between patches or non-overlapping tassel/silking periods. This would require 2-3 weeks difference in planting time. It takes cooperation between neighbors to grow the new sweeter corn types.

Cucumbers - see Vine Crops

Eggplants - see the Tomato Family

Kohlrabi - see Cole Crops

LEAFY VEGETABLE AND SALAD CROPS

Growing tender and sweet leafy vegetables is the mark of a good gardener. Quality in these crops comes from the gardener's ability to supply the water, fertilizer, space and cool temperatures necessary for rapid crop growth. A shortcoming in these needs will result in a strong-flavored, tough crop.

Soils high in organic matter are needed to hold the high supply of nutrients and water. Compost or manures should be added each year to the vegetable bed. Light fertilization and frequent watering promote the rapid growth for tender produce.

These crops love cool soil temperatures. An organic mulch works great to cool the soil, prevent weeds and conserve moisture. You may prefer a sawdust or compost mulch on these leafy vegetables.

Lettuce

Superior-quality leaf and soft head (butter head) lettuce is easy to grow. The iceberg type head lettuce is more difficult in a hot desert climate. To be sweet and tender, lettuce must grow fast. It needs a good supply of water, fertilizer and space.

Lettuce loves cool weather, and will germinate at soil temperatures as low as 35 degrees. It can be one of the first crops to be planted in the spring. Fall lettuce is excellent, coming on in the cool autumn weather. Lettuce is hard to get to germinate when temperatures are above 70 degrees. To get a summer seeding up, cover the bed with a single sheet of newspaper, misting it down lightly twice a day.

In hot weather, lettuce becomes strong flavored and goes to rapid seed formation. Acceptable quality lettuce can be grown in mid-summer, however, with the use of shade cloth over the bed and frequent irrigation.

Lettuce seed is rather tiny, making it a little temperamental in planting. Cover it with only 1/8" to 1/4" of light soil. The seed must be shallow enough to receive ultra-violet light from the moon to germinate.

The most common mistake made with lettuce is planting it too thick. Space the seeds so that excessive thinning will not be necessary. When lettuce becomes crowded, it becomes strong. Start using the crop when it is only an inch or two tall, thinning as you harvest. But you must be careful that the thinning keeps up with the growth. Some seed catalogues offer pelleted seeds; try them. Here the individual seeds are in a coating, increasing their size for easier handling. As plants mature, spacing should expand to 6-9 inches apart.

Popular sweet varieties include "Prizehead," "Buttercrunch," "Crispy Sweet," "Green Ice" and "Tom Thumb."

Spinach

Spinach is nutritious, being high in iron and vitamin A. A favorite salad includes spinach, prizehead lettuce, bacon, sliced eggs and a touch of sweet onion. Spinach can be steamed (just do not overcook it), and can be frozen.

Spinach needs cool weather and is rather frost tolerant, making it a great crop for spring and fall. You can also have good success with summer crops by covering the bed with shade cloth and supplying water frequently.

When it comes to varieties, "Melody" spinach stands out. It has superior sweetness and tenderness.

Swiss Chard

Swiss Chard is a prolific vegetable. Cut it off and in a week it is ready for harvest again. It can be planted any time during the growing season, being tolerant of cool weather and light frosts. It is more tolerant of heat than spinach.

Leaves may grow to 2-3 feet in length. But for best quality, harvest the leaves when they are small and tender, cutting them off an inch or two above the crown.

Chard plants are drought tolerant, heat tolerant and will grow in any soil. But like lettuce and spinach, they need good water and fertilizer and good spacing if you want them tender and sweet. Chard is a member of the beet family and typically comes up in groups. Thin to individual plants at 6-9 inches apart.

While some gardeners object to the red-leaf varieties, claiming it looks too much like beet greens, the red-leaf varieties are sweeter than the standard green.

Celery

While celery is not a leafy vegetable (we eat the stems), its cultural practices fit into the leafy vegetable group. Like lettuce and spinach, it needs a good supply of water and nutrients. If it gets dry it becomes stringy. Years ago, celery was a major crop in Utah. The plant as we know it today, curved to hold cheese, was developed by the Utah State Agricultural College.

Celery is generally transplanted after frost. Start the seeds indoors 12 weeks before planting them outside. The seeds are tiny and require light for germination. In the longer growing-season areas, celery can be direct seeded, planting three weeks before the last spring frost. Place the plants 8-9 inches apart.

Celery requires a steady supply of moisture. Organic matter should be added to the soil to improve the soil's ability to hold water. Never let the celery patch get dry. Celery is also a heavy feeder, so summer application of nitrogen fertilizer (side-dressing) will be needed.

For white stocks, blanch the celery by covering the stems with soil, leaves or paper bags to exclude the light.

Blanching is not necessary; it will improve the flavor, but cuts the nutritional value.

Harvest can start as soon as the plants are big enough. Celery tolerates light frosts. It can be covered with mulching materials and harvested as needed through the fall season.

Leeks - see Onion Family

Lettuce - see Leafy Vegetables

Parsnips - see Root Crops

THE ONION FAMILY

The onion family, including dry onions, green bunching onions, leeks and garlic is easy to grow, but quality in the crop takes a little care. Onions have an inefficient root system compared to other crops. They are poor competitors and must be kept weed free. They are less efficient at extracting soil moisture and need an even water supply to be sweet. Onions are heavy feeders. Cool soils will also promote sweetness. The hint to growing sweet onions is to use a thick organic mulch which cools the soil and stabilizes the moisture.

Dry onions are subject to photoperiodism. That is, the length of the night will tell them when to develop their bulbs. They are classified as "long day" or "short day" varieties. The long day varieties, used in the Mountain West, will start bulbing when the length of the day reaches 14-16 hours, with temperatures above 65 degrees. They will grow leaves until this trigger point is met, then turn to developing the bulbs. To get large bulbs, plant the onions as early as soils allow, growing a lot of leaf before the bulbing starts. The short day varieties are used in southern areas.

Dry onions can be started from seeds, transplants or sets. For long-term storage, seeds are preferred. Transplants should be started indoors 6-8 weeks before planting outside.

Sets are the most popular method for home gardeners. Select firm, small, dormant sets. At planting, sort them

into "larger than a dime" and "smaller than a dime"groups. The larger than a dime group should be harvested first, since they will not store as well. Onions grown from sets will produce seed heads. These heads should be kept plucked off, pushing the plants' growth into the bulbs and not the seeds.

Dry onions are spaced 4-inches apart. The green or bunching onions which are direct seeded should be thinned to 2-inches apart. Garlic, which is planted from sets called cloves, is spaced at 4-6 inches.

Onions may be harvested at any size. For winter storage, harvest the crop after the tops have dried down. They will need good air circulation for at least two weeks while the outer skin cures.

If your family likes soups and chowders, try leeks, the soup onion. They give an excellent mild flavor to soups, stews and sauces. Leeks need the same basic growing care as onions. Direct seed them when the soil warms for early planting. Thin the plants to 3-6 inches apart. Leeks do not bulb like onions, and are mounded with soil or mulch to blanch the lower stem. Like carrots and parsnips, they are best left in the garden into the winter, being harvested as used. Mulch them with straw or sawdust.

PEAS

There are three types of peas common to gardens. The English peas are the common shelled type. The edible-pod peas, also known as sugar peas and snow peas, are the type used in chinese cooking. The pod is picked before the peas inside start to swell. And the newer-type snap peas were developed by plant breeders in Idaho. It produces edible pods with plump tender sweet peas inside. The new snap peas are very heavy producers.

Pea vines vary considerably in height. Dwarf varieties are often planted in double rows to help hold each other up. Taller varieties need a trellis to grow on. Peas can be

planted 2-3 inches apart within the row, or with an equal-distant spacing of 6 inches by 6 inches.

Peas need cool temperatures and will stop bearing when hot weather moves in. Thus, they should be planted as early as the soil allows in the spring. They will germinate at a soil temperature of 40 degrees and will tolerate a light frost. However, pea seeds are very prone to rotting in cold wet soils.

Utah State Agricultural College researchers in Farmington, Utah found that peas are also subject to photo-periodism—the length of the night influences blossoming. In that area, a pea crop planted May 1st will have 50%

fewer pods than a crop planted April 1st—another reason for early planting.

Peas have a low need for nitrogen fertilizers. They perform best on a soil rich in organic matter. Pea flowers are self-pollinating, that is they do not require insects for pollination.

Peas are harvested as the pods fill out, and they should be picked every few days. Allowing peas to oversize will cut their sweetness and decrease the vines' production. Peas will be sweeter if harvested during the cool morning hours, before the day's heat comes on. Edible-pod peas should be harvested before the peas fill out; their pods become fibrous if allowed to mature.

Suggested English pea varieties include "Lincoln," "Early Frosty," "Patriot," and "Banquet." Suggested edible-pod pea varieties include "Oregon Sugar Pod," "Little Sweetie," and "Mammoth Melting Sugar." Suggested snap-pea varieties include "Sugar Ann," "Sugar Snap," and "Sugar Daddy."

Peppers - see the Tomato Family

POTATOES

The best advice for growing potatoes is to use "certified seed." This certification indicates that Department of Agriculture inspectors found the potato growing field disease free. It does not prevent disease, but greaty reduces the chances. Gardeners often plant left-overs or grocery store potatoes, unaware of the serious disease problems they may be propagating. Many of the potato diseases live in the soil, so do not replant potatoes in a patch where disease problems have occurred.

To get the potatoes off to a good start, cut the seed potatoes into 1 1/2- to 2-inch cubes. Smaller pieces will not give the young plant the vigor needed to take off rapidly. Small seed potatoes will not need cutting. Potatoes may be planted when the soil temperature reaches 50 degrees (measured at 8 o'clock in the morning at 4-inches deep). This is generally a couple of weeks before the last average spring frost date. Potatoes are generally planted 4 inches deep with a spacing of 12-15" by 12-15". Rows should be placed close enough together to shade the soil. Cool soils grow sweeter potatoes.

The spacing will determine the size of the potatoes. Each garden and each variety may need some adjustment in spacing to achieve the desired potatoes size. If your potatoes get too big by fall, reduce the spacings; if they are too small, increase your spacing a touch next year.

A potato plant produces roots from the seed piece down and stems from the seed piece up. The potatoes are actually storage stem tissues, and thus form from the seed piece up. If they grow on the surface where they receive sunlight, they will turn green. Green potatoes are mildly poisonous, and should not be used. To prevent greening, potatoes are hilled; soil is mounded up around the plant when it is 6-12 inches tall. In block planting, where there are no walkways, you can use 6 inches of straw as hilling material. The straw will also control the weeds and cool the soil.

Potatoes are fussy about a steady supply of water. If they get a little dry, growth of the tubers is stopped. And when water is reapplied, the growth takes off from the tuber eyes. This restart will result in knobby tubers.

Potatoes are heavy feeders of nitrogen, phosphorus and potassium. Nitrogen stress is very common in home gardens during August and September. It shows as yellowing of the leaves and early die-back of the vines. (Vines should remain green until about frost time.) Potatoes need a nitrogen sidedressing applied in mid summer to keep them going. (See "fertilizers" for details.) If potatoes are over-fertilized at the start of the season they will become excessively viney, suppressing tuber development. The key in fertilizing potatoes is to do it lightly and often.

Potatoes can be dug as soon as they are large enough to eat. A common mistake gardeners make in harvesting potatoes for fall storage is digging them too early. Cool fall weather must move in before you have suitable storage conditions.

For fall storage, dig the potatoes a couple of weeks after frost kills the vines. Be careful not to cut or damage the tubers when digging. Tubers which are accidentally nicked should not be placed in storage. Dirt should be brushed off. The potatoes need to be cured for two weeks by keeping them in the dark, at 60-75 degrees. The ideal storage temperature is 40 degrees. Potatoes will sprout if stored above 50 degrees. If stored below 35 degrees the potato becomes sweet. This sweetness can somewhat be reversed by holding the potatoes near room temperature for a couple of weeks before using them. Potatoes must be stored in the dark to prevent greening.

"Red Pontiac" is the most popular variety, out-producing other varieties. Some cooks don't like it due to its deepset eyes. "Norland" and "LaSoda" are also good red varieties. The most popular white varieties are "Norgold Russet," "Kennebeck," and "Butte."

Pumpkins - see Vine Crops

Spinach - see Leafy Vegetables

Swiss Chard - see Leafy Vegetables

Radishes - see Root Crops

RHUBARB

Rhubarb is an easy-to-grow cool-weather perennial. Its stalks are used in sauces, pies and fruit drinks. It freezes well for off-season use. The leaves are poisonous.

Rhubarb is propagated by dividing dormant, 3+ year-old crowns. Split the crowns between the large buds or "eyes," leaving as large a piece of storage root as possible with each large bud. A large crown can be split into 4 to 8 pieces. When old crowns are used, only the vigorous outer portions should be planted. Hills should be divided and reset about every eight years; otherwise, they become too thick, producing only slender stocks. Be sure to protect the roots from dehydrating during the transplant process.

Rhubarb is best transplanted in the fall, after the tops have been killed by frost. It may also be planted in the early spring. Place the crown pieces 2-4 feet apart, covering them with 2-3 inches of soil.

Rhubarb will thrive in almost any type of soil that is rich in organic matter and well drained. It likes the sun but will not tolerate heat nor full shade. In the Intermountain West's warmer valleys, a site which provides good morning sun but a little shade relief from the summer afternoon heat is ideal.

Before growth starts in the spring fertilize with 1/3-1/2 cup of ammonium sulfate (21-0-0) or equivalent around each plant. An annual application of compost as a mulch is desirable to control weeds. Rhubarb is a poor competitor and should be kept weed free. Any cultivation around the plant should be shallow to avoid damaging the root system.

Poor coloring of stalks may come from too much shade, too hot a location, water problems or poor varieties. Rhubarb is sensitive to over watering, which leads to *Phytophthora* Crown Rot. Other insect and disease problems seldom warrant treatments.

Heavy production is dependent upon a strong leaf growth the previous summer. The harvest period is short, generally about two months in the late spring. When the weather turns hot, stop harvesting and allow the plants to grown naturally. Cut off seed stalks as soon as they arise. Do not harvest the first year after planting and keep the second year's harvest small.

Harvest the largest and best stalks by grasping them near the base and pulling them slightly to one side. Cutting off the stalks can damage the crown. This thinning permits better growth of the remaining smaller stalks. Never remove more than 1/4 of the plant at one time.

Popular varieties include "Canada Red," "Ruby" and "Valentine."

ROOT CROPS

The key to raising superior root crops is an even supply of moisture. Produce will become strong and stringy if the soil is allowed to dry out. They like soil rich in decayed organic matter which holds their needed water. But they dislike fresh organic materials and manures, which lead to root splitting and rough surfaces. Compost the materials before adding them to the root crop bed.

Root crops prefer a cool soil; an organic mulch which keeps the soil cooler in the summer heat leads to sweeter crops. The mulch also helps to stabilize the moisture level and to control weeds.

Carrots

The hint for sweet carrots is to pay attention to the variety. Carrots are high in oils, and in most varieties the oil becomes strong tasting. "Scarlet Nantes" and "Pioneer" are excellent varieties which hold a very sweet, crispy taste through the winter.

Carrot seeds are small and many gardeners have a hard time getting them to germinate. Cover the seeds very lightly, and keep them moist. On heavy soils, cover the seed with a little sand or peat moss to prevent surface crusting. Carrots can be planted from when the soil warms in the spring through mid-summer. In warm weather, soil surface temperatures may be too hot for seed germination. Cover the carrot bed with a newspaper to shade and cool the seed. You can easily sprinkle over the paper to supply moisture.

Crowding will reduce root size. Be sure to check for doubles when thinning the young plants. Thin the roots to 2-3 inches apart. Stress caused by uneven moisture or hot soil temperature will cause stubbiness, knobbyness and splitting.

Straw is used to mulch carrots, parsnips and leeks which are stored in the garden for the winter. The crops are dug as needed through the winter. This type of storage promotes a sweet crispy crop. (Photo by David Whiting)

When carrot roots poke their shoulders through the soil surface, the shoulder will green up, reducing the sweetness. To prevent this keep a good mulch over the bed.

Carrots store superbly through the winter if left in the garden and mulched with straw or sawdust. They actually improve in sweetness and crispness as the soil cools. Dig a panful as you use them.

Beets

For quality in beet greens or beet roots, harvest them when they're young. Do not allow the crop to overmature. If you enjoy beet greens, make multiple plantings through the growing season.

When thinning beets, watch for doubles. Beet have 3-4 seeds per cluster, so they take a little extra care in thinning. Thin the plants to 3-6" apart.

"Detroit Dark Red" is the standard variety, universal in planting. Some other good varieties include "Pacemaker II," "Earlisweet," and "Warrior." "Golden Beet," which is yellow in color, is exceptionally sweet.

Parsnips

Parsnips are not a popular vegetable, but are a favorite in many households. Home-grown parsnips, which arc left in the garden into the winter to cool and sweeten, are marvelous. Enjoy them baked with a roast like potatoes and carrots, or stir fried.

Parsnips are planted as the soil warms in the spring, generally a couple of weeks before the last spring frost. They are a little difficult to get up, taking 2-3 weeks to germinate. Like other root crops, be careful not to over cover the seed. On heavy soils, covering the seed with sand or peat moss will help prevent soil crusting. Parsnip seeds have a short shelf life, only 2-3 years. Space seeds

evenly to prevent excessive thinning, and then thin them to 6-inches apart.

Parsnips need some cool fall weather to improve flavor and sweetness before harvesting. Leave them in the garden into the winter, mulching them from extreme cold with straw or sawdust.

"All America" and "Model" are excellent varieties.

Radishes

Like the other root crops, the secret to sweet radishes is a good even supply of moisture. If they get dry, they get hot. Radishes like cool temperatures, and do excellently in spring and fall plantings. Under shade cloth and with frequent waterings, you also can grow a good crop through the summer. Radishes only take 3 to 4 weeks to mature, so plant a very small crop every 2-3 weeks. Radishes will not fatten their roots if they're crowded. Being quick maturing, they must be thinned shortly after emerging.

There are many good varieties of radishes on the market. A favorite is the small round roots of "Burpee White." It is always sweet and mild.

Turnips & Rutabagas

Turnips and Rutabagas are grown for greens (leaves) and for roots. Harvest them young for best quality. Rutabagas are a cross between cabbage and turnips, and generally give larger roots than turnips. Like the other root crops, they need a constant supply of moisture and a soil high in organic matter. Tolerating cool weather, they are one of the first crops to be planted. Thin the plants to 4-6 inches.

"Tokyo Cross Hybrid" is an excellent, quick-maturing turnip. Other good varieties include "Market Express Hybrid," "White Lady Hybrid" and "DeNancy."

THE TOMATO FAMILY

Tomatoes, peppers and eggplants, being cousins, need the same basic care in watering, fertilizing and planting. Yields are heavily impacted by their care and by the weather.

Tomatoes

Tomatoes are America's most popular vegetable, being found in most home gardens. They may be grown from transplants or direct seeded. Gardeners prefer transplants to get a jump on the season. The ideal transplant is 6-8 weeks old, dark green, 6-10 inches tall, with a stocky stem and good root system. But you will rarely find it in the nursery. Tomatoes don't grow in the greenhouse on rainy days, and can grow several inches a week in sunny weather.

Larger tomato plants, which may be a little overgrown, have the advantage when being transplanted into less then beautiful weather. With their slowed growth rate they are more tolerant of wind and of rainy weather. The key to

success with the larger plants is to plant the tomato deep. Leave the top six inches sticking out and bury the rest. The buried stem develops roots quickly, and the plant jumps into rapid growth. To keep the plant in the warmer soils near the surface, dig a trench four inches deep and bury the stem in a near-horizontal position. A water-soluble fertilizer (root stimulator) should be applied to signal the plant to start growing again.

If the tomato transplant is a little smaller than the ideal size, it is likely in a rapidly growing state and is ready to take off. These tender plants will need protection from wind and from cold. They also like a water-soluble fertilizer (root stimulator) applied at planting (see "fertilizers").

A tomato which is short and rather thick stemmed (fatter than a pen) has probably been treated with a hormone to control growth. Avoid them, they may be slow to take off in the garden.

Tomatoes should not be planted outside without protection until summer weather moves in, generally two weeks after the average spring frost date; about the time the apple trees show the first little green apples. Tomatoes will not tolerate frost and need daytime temperatures consistently above 60 degrees. A week of temperatures below 50 degrees will stunt the plants and reduce yields. If this occurs, give your tomatoes a shot in the arm with a water soluble fertilizer application applied when summer weather returns.

Researchers have found no advantage to crowding tomatoes, you can fit in extra plants but it will not increase yields, and the denser foliage will increase disease problems. For trellised tomatoes, minimum spacing is 24 inches. Non-staked tomatoes should be planted at 36-48 inch spacing. The small vine patio types can be planted at 12-inch spacings.

Black plastic mulch is superb for tomatoes. It warms the soil, pushing the crop and increasing yields. The plastic will also control weeds and stabilize the soil moisture. See mulches for details on planting in plastic mulch. One summer in Twin Falls Idaho, the author ran out of plastic when it came time to plant the tomatoes. Only half of the tomato row was mulched. That summer, August was cool. The mulched tomatoes were in production by late July, but the un-mulched vines had no red fruit until early September!

Trellis your tomatoes. It makes the fruit easy to pick, keeps the fruit off the ground, and conserves space. The standard tomato cage is fine only for the small vine varieties. For the common indeterminate-type varieties, the American Horticultural Society recommends a trellis 24 inches across and 5 feet high. A 6-foot section of concrete reinforcing mesh or similar fencing materials makes a great cage. Cut off the bottom cross wire and stick it in the ground.

Tomatoes can also be trained on a single pole or tied to a fence, but this takes a lot of extra labor. A one-inch strip of nylon pantyhose makes great soft ties. When training tomatoes to a single pole, prune off the side shoots weekly.

Tomatoes love a little fertilizer, but just a little. If over fed with nitrogen, they go into vine growth at the expense of fruiting. For this reason, many gardeners are afraid to fertilize them, but they like a little. At transplanting, apply a water-soluble feed (root stimulator) according to label directions. One to three applications can be made, depending on what other fertilizer has been added.

A light nitrogen application applied during fruiting will increase yields. Make this application just as the first fruits begin to turn. Additional applications can be made every 3-4 weeks. The fertilizer can be the water-soluble type (see label direction). Or a dry granular like ammonium nitrate or ammonium sulfate can be used. Sprinkle one tablespoon per plant around and water it in.

Tomatoes are fussy about watering. They like an even supply of moisture. A water imbalance will show as

Blossom End Rot, that common black leather spot on the bottom of the fruit, (see "Diseases-tomato").

Tomatoes are pollinated by plant movement (wind). Temperatures will influence this process. Flowers which open following a cool night, below 55 degrees, will not have viable pollen. This is why the early varieties are not always earlier, and why tomatoes often quit producing in the fall. This lack of production can be corrected by using the tomato blossom set sprays. Blossoms will also abort when temperatures reach above 95 degrees by 10:00 o'clock in the morning.

When the fruit seems slow to ripen, hold back on the watering a bit. This stress will enhance the ripening process, but can cut yields. This technique is particularly helpful to mature the fruit as the season draws near the end.

Tomato flavor is best when temperatures are 75 to 90 degrees. Tomatoes ripening under cooler temperatures will be softer and more bland in flavor. Some varieties are specially bred for production in cooler climates. These quick maturing, cool climate varieties are definitely lacking in flavor, compared to the standard tomatoes. However, in the cooler high mountain valleys, these cool-season varieties are still better than store-bought tomatoes.

As the growing season ends, many gardeners like to bring in the last of the tomatoes for ripening indoors. This is an easy process, but what works best for your specific home is learned by trial and error.

Store only the fruit from vigorous vines. Fruit from spent vines will not have the flavor. Pick the ripening fruit and the mature green (full size) fruit. Fruit should be picked before a frost (32 degrees). Or if daytime temperatures drop below 50 degrees for more the four days, pick the fruit. The stems should be removed to prevent puncturing. The fruit should be gently washed and allowed to air dry. Hand drying can scratch the skin, allowing for disease problems.

Ripening fruit should be sorted weekly from green fruit. As a tomato ripens, it releases ethylene gas, which will stimulate the ripening of the others. A mature green tomato takes two weeks to ripen at 65-70 degrees, but at 55 degrees it will take 3-4 weeks. Lower temperatures will lengthen the storage life but will decrease the flavor.

The trick to storing tomatoes is getting the humidity right. A generation ago, people had root cellars which worked great, but today most homes are not so equipped. If the humidity in the storage area is too low, the tomatoes shrivel up. If the humidity is too high, the tomatoes mold. What works in any given home is learned somewhat by trial and error.

Tomatoes could be kept on a shelf or in a box in a cool moist fruit room or basement. To increase the humidity, fruit can be individually wrapped in newspapers or wax paper, or the fruit can be placed in small groups in plastic bags. When using bags, be sure to cut a few air holes so they can breathe. You can have good success by placing the fruit in a blanching pan. The rack holds the fruit up out of a bit of water in the bottom. Some have success with pulling the entire vine and hanging it in a cool moist shed.

Your indoor-ripened tomatoes will not be nearly as flavorful as the summer vine-ripe fruit. But compare it to the grocery-store tomato and you will be proud of your crop.

When it comes to varieties there are a lot of options and a lot of opinions. World-wide over 2,000 varieties are grown. Tomato varieties can be grouped by fruit size, vine size or primary use.

Vines are classified as "determinate," "indeterminate," and "patio." Determinate types are preferred for commercial production because they produce a large yield over a short time. Many of the new determinate canners have only one large picking. Vines on determinate varieties are medium in size, and vine growth is determined or stopped as the plant reaches the fruiting stage.

Indeterminate varieties are more popular with home gardeners. They continue in full production until fall weather takes them out. Vines are large, continuing to grow through the season. The vines of patio varieties stay small, suitable for planting in a container on the patio.

Variety names or descriptions often indicate disease resistance, such as "VFNT." The V indicates resistance to Verticillium Disease, the F indicates resistance to Fusarium Disease. The N indicates resistance to nematodes, which are a serious problem only in warmer soil areas. T indicates resistance to Tobacco Mosaic Virus. Disease resistance is standard in the newer varieties.

Listed here are the most popular varieties asked for in the store.

Beefmaster VFN — 80 days from transplant. Possibly the best of the Beefsteak types with giant-size fruits up to 2 pounds. Typical of giant fruit types, it is slower to produce and has low yields.

Celebrity VFNT — 70 days from transplant. This is an All American Selection with a strong determinate vine. Its large, 8-ounce firm fruits resist cracking.

Deloro VFN — 72 days from transplant. This variety is a big hit with the commercial growers for its extra heavy yields over a short harvest period. The plant is so loaded with the medium-sized fruits it looks red. The very meaty fruit is great for sauces but too dry for juice. It has determinate vines.

Early Girl — 55 days from transplant. The author always plants an Early Girl for his early table use and canning. The large indeterminate vine produces an abundance of small-medium size fruits. The extra-heavy yields from Early Girl are amazing.

Jet Star VF — 72 days from transplant. This is a heavy producer of large crack-free fruit. It has compact, sturdy, indeterminate vines. The fruit has a great vine-ripe flavor, is meaty, sweet and has lower acid than most varieties. Add lemon juice when canning Jet Star.

Roma VF — 76 days from transplant. This variety has small pear-shaped fruit with a meaty interior which has few seeds. This paste tomato is popular for home canning. It has determinate vines.

Super Fantastic — 72 days from transplant. It's indeterminate vines set large, firm fruit, resistant to cracking. It is noted for high yields and season-long production.

Sweet 100 — 65 days from transplant. This is the most popular tomato in the world. It grows cherry-sized tomatoes in clusters like grapes. It is noted for its tender skin and extra-sweet fruit. One plant will keep a family for the summer.

Sweet 100 is the most popular tomato variety in the world. A typical plant produces around 500 exceptionally sweet cherry sized tomatoes with tender skins. (Photo by David Whiting)

Peppers

Peppers need the same care in watering and fertilizing as tomatoes. They are even more prone to yield reduction from being planted too early or from being planted in a cool rainy week. Peppers are spaced at 18 inches and are not trellised.

The best-selling bell pepper varieties include "Better Bell," "Yolo Wonder," "Valley Giant Hybrid," "Big Bertha," "Bell Boy," and "Park's Whopper." "Gypsy Hybrid" and "Sweet Banana" are excellent sweet yellow peppers. "Anaheim," "Cayenne" and "Jalapeno" are the most popular hot peppers.

Eggplant

Eggplant has the same cultural practices as tomatoes and peppers. Eggplants are typically spaced at 18-24 inches and are not trellised.

Popular eggplant varieties include "Dusky Hybrid," "Early Royal Hybrid," "Ichiban Hybrid," "Black Bell," "Burpee Hybrid," and "Classic."

Squash - see Vine Crops   **Turnips - see Root Crops**

The yields of peppers (left) and eggplant (right) will be reduced if planted too early, in cool weather. (Photo by David Whiting)

VINE CROPS

Vine crops have the same cultural requirements and will be discussed as a group. They like warm summer weather and yields will be reduced if planted in cold spring temperatures.

These crops, which spread over the ground, are ideal for black plastic mulch. The plastic controls weeds and conserves moisture. But the big advantage of plastic mulch is earlier production and heavier yields. The plastic warms the soil, pushing the crop. In unusually warm seasons, response will not be dramatic. But in cool summers and in the higher cooler valleys, crops can be pushed ahead 2-4 weeks!

Vine crops can be started by direct seeding or from transplants. With the warmth of the plastic mulch, a direct-seeded crop will germinate in just a few days. Direct seedings will give higher yields. Vine crop roots suberize readily when disturbed, that is they develop a scar-like tissue which reduces the roots' effectiveness. Transplants must be handled carefully. They should be young and not pot bound. Start the transplants 2-4 weeks before planting them outside. A water-soluble fertilizer (root stimulator) should be used on transplants.

Summer squash and cucumbers can be direct seeded when apples reach full bloom, around the time of the average spring frost. Hold off on planting the others and on all transplants a couple of weeks. They do best when planted in warm summer weather. A week of day-time temperatures below 55 degrees will stunt the plants and cut yields. If this should occur, a light application of a water-soluble fertilizer will be helpful.

Cool winds will quickly wither the tender leaves of young vine crops. Cucumbers are particularly sensitive to a cool breeze which turns the leaf margins brown. Gardeners could avoid having to plant and replant the vine crops if they would take a little precaution. Again, don't plant too early, nor plant in a storm. Placing something to the side of the plant to block the wind can be a great help. Boards, buckets, bricks, and boxes work well. A friend uses a leafy branch of lilac and reports good success.

Vine crops are typically planted in hills, allowing 3-4 plants to grow from a single spot. The hills are generally spaced every 3-4 feet. Higher yields can be achieved by thinning the crops to one plant per spot, with a plant every 12-18 inches. The plants get better distribution of water and nutrients this way.

Vine crops are low nitrogen feeders. If over fertilized they will go into excessive vine growth at the expense of fruiting. They like a soil high in organic matter, with its increased water-holding ability.

Vine crops have male and female flowers. The larger male flowers are generally the first to appear. Female flowers have a tiny fruit at their base. Insect activity is required to move the pollen from the male flower to the female flower. Where bee activity is limited, gardeners may need to assist in this necessary function. Pollen can be transferred by a water color brush. But it is easy just to pick a male blossom, remove its petals and touch the center of the female blooms with the center of the male bloom. Where hand pollination is needed, mid-morning is the best time. Fruit on female flowers which are not pollinated will start to grow but will abort quickly (see "Diseases-Vine Crops-Blossom Drop").

Vine crops have male and female blossoms. Pollen must be transferred from the male flower to the female flower for the fruit to develop. (left) — The female blooms have a small fruit at their base. The male blooms (lower in the picture) come on slender stems. (right) — A bee is gathering pollen. In gardens where bee activity is limited, man must assist the pollination work to get a crop. (Photos by David Whiting)

Cucumbers

There are many types of cucumbers; for general home use they are classified into pickling and slicing types. For optimum quality, they are not interchangeable. "Burpless" cucumbers are slicers specially bred for their mild flavor and fewer seeds. Many of the newer varieties are "gyno-ecious," that is they produce cucumbers from the all-female blossoms.

The occasional bitterness in cukes is caused by a compound known as Cucurbitacin. It will vary within individual fruits and is found just under the skin. Its occurrence is related to stress and varieties. Extreme heat or cool weather will promote it. Stress from water, wind, fertilizer, etc. will promote it. Some varieties are very prone to it. The burpless slicing varieties have been bred to be less bitter.

Consider trellising your cucumbers. Trellising conserves space and makes them easier to pick. They do not naturally climb, and must be trained up the trellis fence. If cucumbers are allowed to mature on the vines (by intent or by missing some when picking), production will slow or even stop.

Popular pickling varieties include "Bush Pickle," "Calypso Hybrid," "Wisconsin SMR 18," and "Liberty Hybrid." Popular standard slicers include "Dusky Hybrid," "Sweet Slice Hybrid" and "Marketmore." The recommended burpless mild slicers include "Burpless Hybrid," "Euro-American," "Sweet Success" and "Jet Set Hybrid." There are also many good compact vine varieties including "Pot Luck Hybrid," "Bush Champion Hybrid" and "Salad Bush Hybrid."

Squash and Pumpkins

Summer squash are those varieties which can be harvested immature, with soft skins. Zucchini is the most popular type. If they are allowed to oversize on the vine, production will be slowed or stopped. For exceptional summer squash, harvest them while very small and avoid over-cooking them.

Winter squash are those varieties which are harvested when the rind is hard and are held for winter storage. Immature winter squash will be watery and lacking in flavor.

Winter squash and pumpkins need the full growing season to mature a hard rind. Maturity can be determined by pressing the thumbnail into the fruit's skin. If the skin is hard and impervious to scratching, the fruit is fully matured and will store well. Those squash with softer rinds should be used first.

Cut winter squash and pumpkins off the vine, leaving one inch of stem. This stem piece helps suppress fruit rot in storage. When frost kills the vines, the fruit should be harvested; growth is stopped at this point. Pumpkins which are green will turn (ripen) in storage.

The list of squash varieties is long, and each family has their favorites. Many popular types are now available with compact vines.

Popular Zucchini varieties include "Zucchini Elite Hybrid," "Spineless Zucchini Hybrid," "Black Jack" and "Parks' Green Whopper." "Dixie Hybrid," "Butterbar Hybrid" and "Gold Rush" are excellent yellow summer squash varieties. "Peter Pan Hybrid" and "Sunburst Hybrid" are good patty pan types.

There are many types of winter squash. "Buttercup" is good. It has a small rounded fruit, and the entire squash can be cooked at once. It is extra sweet and mild textured. "Sweet Mama" and "Sweet Meat" are also good small-sized winter squash. Other gardeners prefer "Butternut," "Pink Banana," and "Hubbard."

Try Spaghetti squash. It can be used in the summer or stored for winter. When cooked it comes out in long strands like spaghetti. Enjoy it with spaghetti sauce, mushroom gravy or cheese sauce on it.

Squash is one vegetable that is readily over cooked. Try Zucchini quick cooked in a stir-fry fashion; it does not take long. Microwave cooking is excellent for winter squash.

Cantaloupes and Watermelons

Harvest cantaloupes when they reach the full slip stage, that is when the stem pops off with just slight pressure.

If you are not growing excellent cantaloupes, look at your varieties. Cantaloupe varieties vary considerably in quality. The sweetest varieties often have soft flesh, and the firmer flesh ones may be lacking in sweetness. Here are some of the best. The new "Pulsar Hybrid" is a favorite. Its fruit is large, sweet and firm, and it holds well on the vine. "Sweet Dream" is excellent with a sweet green flesh. Other popular varieties include "Summit Hybrid," "Harper Hybrid," "Classic Hybrid," and "Ambrosia Hybrid." "Early Dew," "Jade Dew" and "Rocky Sweet" are good muskmelon types.

Watermelons are difficult to judge at the perfect harvest state. Sound is a good method. Each variety each season will have a particular ring to it at harvest time. Thump the melon. A ring indicates immaturity, a dull thud indicates readiness or over maturity. As the melon reaches maturity the surface will dull. The ground color (the non-green area where it lies on the ground) will change from a straw color to a yellow. With a little pressure, the melon will partially detach from the vine.

Like cantaloupes, the key to good watermelons is the right variety. "Crimson Sweet Watermelon" is tops; being a rounded, medium-size melon with superb sweetness.

Watermelons - see Vine Crops

If you are not growing excellent-quality cantaloupes and watermelons, check your varieties. These rounded Crimson Sweet Watermelons are tops in flavor and sweetness. (Photo by David Whiting)

8
Insects and Diseases

The most frustrating thing a gardener deals with is fighting insects and diseases. There is so much folk lore about pest control that gardeners are often stumped about what is effective.

At one end of the spectrum is the gardener who routinely sprays everything every couple of weeks. Research suggests that this practice will increase insect problems by 500% plus! The heavy blanket spraying upsets the natural balance of control; beneficial insects and insect predators are suppressed or destroyed.

At the other end is the organic gardener who uses no so called "insecticides." Understand, however, that *any* product used to control insects, whether man-made or natural, is an "insecticide." Many of the so-called "organic" control agents are slow to break down in the environment, creating a greater toxicity hazard that the chemical "insecticides" organic gardeners are avoiding.

A middle-of-the-road organic approach appears to be the most practical solution. The extensive study, "Report and Recommendations on Organic Farming," by the United States Department of Agriculture, will support this limited, but justifiable-need approach to chemical use.

The following suggestions explain the author's approach to pest control:

1. Always start by identifying the crop(s) and pest. Do not just spray; the pest may be controllable by other measures or by other chemicals. Identifying what crops are affected will greatly reduce the possibilities to look at.

Insect problems are usually identifiable by finding the insects present. You may need to look carefully to find the pests. Look on the underside of leaves or near the crown of the plant where many insects hide. Do not forget to look at night; many common pests are nocturnal (night feeders). Insects typically feed by eating the plant (consuming it), or by sucking on the sap (leaves become sticky and twisted).

Disease problems are more difficult to identify. They are diagnosed by what is abnormal with the plant. Typical symptoms include cankers (sores), blights (die backs), wilts, leaf spots, etc. Some disease problems are caused by fungus, bacteria or viruses. Of these "parasitic" diseases only a few are controllable by fungicide sprays. "Non-parasitic" diseases are caused by environmental factors such as wind, water problems, sunburn, fertilizer problems, frost, etc. Sprays are not useful in controlling non-parasitic diseases.

2. Is the pest likely to threaten the success of the crop? Some insects may be just passing through. The damage may be done before the problem is noticed. Many insects may be present but are not actually a threat to the crop. Other pests need immediate action to prevent the problem from exploding.

3. What options are practical for control? Many insects and most diseases are controlled by cultural methods. However, some of the common "organic" control procedures are not practical. Many control procedures are preventative, not curative.

4. When a pesticide is needed, carefully determine what should be used and how it should be applied. When applying pesticides, treat only the infected crop and avoid blanket sprays. Many pesticides have environmental factors which should be considered before they are used. A serious consideration for home gardeners to look at is bee kill. *As a gardener, you have the responsibility to protect these valuable pollinating insects!* There is no blanket spray effective for all problems.

The author uses few pesticides. In a year he typically uses less than a pint of spray concentrate per season. This is because he has a healthy natural control program in effect. Research from the Seattle area suggests that it takes 5-plus years for mother nature to shift back into control following the overuse of chemicals.

Reduce pesticide usage through choosing effective methods of application. The typical hose-end sprayer is fast and easy. But research finds that hose-end sprayers, even at their best, are rather inaccurate in dilution and somewhat ineffective in the control achieved. On the other hand, you have excellent control over mixing and coverage with the pump-up tank sprayer. These take a little more time, but use only a fraction of the pesticide. I have found much superior control with tank sprayers. With a hose-end sprayer, you will use more spray in a single application than you will likely use in a entire year in a tank sprayer.

Another factor influencing the environmental hazard of a pesticide is its formulation. Sprays, which are made to stick to the plant, present a lower environmental hazard than dust. Bees will mistakenly pick up dust as pollen.

COMMON VEGETABLE INSECTS AND DISEASES

The following is a reference guide to the common and occasional insect and disease problems found in vegetable gardens in the Intermountain West.

The first section includes general feeders—those insects which are common on a wide variety of crops. The second section lists the common insect and disease problems by crops.

Brief descriptions and pictures are included to assist in identifying the pests. A summary of the life cycle is given to help in your control strategy. Many gardeners will be surprised to learn that recurring problems may be coming from the weed patch or the unplowed fall garden! The guide indicates times of the season to watch for the various pests.

In discussing control options, standard non-chemical control procedures are listed. Indication is given as to whether the insect is a common, routine pest, or one which just shows up occasionally. Those pests which need immediate attention to prevent the problem from exploding are particularly identified.

When it comes to pesticides, all the options have been listed, but suggestions are given to help the gardener make a wise selection. Many of the recommendations are adapted from pest control research done for commercial growers. Preference has been given to biological control agents which have low environmental hazard and low human toxicity.

One of the unique things about this book is that the author has indicated situations when sprays present a known environmental hazard such as bee kill, spider mite build-up or bird kill. Many gardeners will be surprised to find that their old standard spray may be seriously impacting the environment. These problems are listed to help the gardener make a educated choice in his spray program.

The "Application to Harvest Period" is the number of days following the applications of a chemical on a crop before the crop can be harvested for use. The days are set by the government from actual measurements of the pesticide residue on the crop. It varies for each crop and each pesticide. Washing the crop will not reduce this period. Care should be taken that using a spray does not interfere with the harvest of the vegetables.

COMMON GARDEN INSECTS

Aphids

Aphids are the most common pest found in the garden. World wide, there are several thousand different species, with some 400-plus species occurring in the Intermountain West. Most of the common garden plants can be attacked by some species of aphid. Aphids are host specific, that is each species has a limited range of plants it will attack.

With all the different kinds, aphids vary in appearance and life history. But generally speaking, aphids are small, up to 3/16 inch, tear-dropped shaped, soft bodied, and may or may not have wings. Wingless aphids are most common, but many species will develop a winged generation when the food supply dwindles or the population becomes crowded.

Aphids are generally black, green or yellowish. But don't be surprised to find aphids in white, gray, red, pink, blue, brown or other interesting color combinations.

One of the easiest ways to identify most aphids is their two "tail-pipe" like structures, technically called cornicles, sticking out the back of their lower abdomen. They may be short, just two bumps, or rather long, looking somewhat like antennae, but most aphids have them. On smaller species, you may need a small hand lens or magnifying glass to check this characteristic.

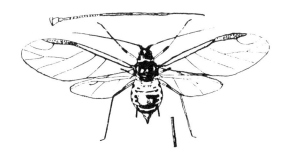 

Typical Aphid shape. (Left) Winged adult Green Peach Aphid. (Right) Wingless adult Green Peach Aphid. (U.S.D.A.)

Some aphids, like the cabbage aphid, are coated with a fine waxy powder. Others, like the Woolly Apple Aphid, hide under a coat of wool-like wax. These cottony looking spots can easily be mistaken for a fungus growth. Their waxy coating protects them from insecticides and predators, making them somewhat difficult to control.

Aphid populations often appear to explode overnight. A large migration of winged pests can move in. Aphids multiply rapidly, usually reproducing parthenogenetically (without mating). The females of many species are capable of giving birth to live young. Always keep an eye open for these pests; they seem to appear out of nowhere.

Most species of aphids spend the winter in the egg stage. Aphids feed by sucking plant fluids, damaging the plant from the excessive draw on sap. Plants can be stunted, turn yellow or wilt; leaves may drop prematurely. Fruit size and quality may be reduced, yields may be hurt. Aphids are also a means of disease spread, particularly virus diseases.

Leaves often become sticky from their "honeydew," the sappy excretion of the aphid. You can spot aphids on cherries and maples while driving down the street, just from the dripping leaves. Ants and other insects love to feed on this honeydew. When you see ants climbing on a plant, it is an indication that the plant has aphids. Occasionally, black, sooty mold will grow on the sticky mess.

Leaves which are curled, cupped or twisted are often a sign of aphids. Gardeners with snowballs or plums find this common in the spring from aphids feeding as the leaves start to unfold. In July, the common Black Cherry Aphid can curl the cherry leaves in just a few days. This leaf twisting provides excellent protection for the pest; many predators can't find them and sprays won't reach them. Whenever you diagnose a twisted or cupped leaf, look first for aphids inside. This procedure saves a lot of time in diagnosing plant problems.

Some plants will form a gall in response to aphid feeding. A common example of this is the Cooley Spruce Gall Aphid which causes a pine cone-looking gall where it feeds on spruce. This pest is also an example of an alternate host aphid, spending half of it's life on spruce and half on Douglas Fir. To sum it all up, aphids are a large and complex superfamily of insect pests.

Controlling Aphids

Aphid populations are usually kept in bounds by predators, parasites, aphid diseases and the weather. During many years ladybug populations have kept the aphids under control. The common predators include the ladybugs, lacewings and the larvae of some syrphid flies. Braconids and chalcid flies are common parasites. Sub-zero winter temperatures will help kill wintering eggs.

(Left) Ladybug larvae feeding on aphids. Spring aphid populations are often kept in bounds by these predators. (Right) Ants protect aphids from predators and feed on the aphids' sticky honeydew. Ants climbing on plants are a good sign of aphids. (Photos: U.S.D.A. Extension Service)

As all gardeners know, aphid populations do get out of hand from time to time. Always keep your eye open for aphids, and for their predators. Predator populations build slowly following an aphid explosion, but there have been many times where ladybug larvae have caught up in their spring-time control, without the use of insecticides.

Migrating aphids may be attracted and captured in yellow pans of water (add a few drops of detergent to help catch the pest) or on yellow sticky traps. It has also been reported that reflection off aluminum foil, placed under the plants, will help repel them.

Aphids may be dislodged from sturdy plants by a forceful hosing down. Some may be killed but others will simply move back. Adding a little soap to the water may improve results, but remember that the soaps, being slower to break down, may be more hazardous to the environment than insecticides. These organic control methods may help reduce populations, but generally will not stop an explosion.

Under heavy population pressures, aphids need insecticidal sprays for effective control. Quick action will be needed on plants where leaves will curl, thus protecting the aphids. Most common garden sprays are effective on most aphids. *Sevin* is generally not too effective on aphids. Systemic insecticides, which aphids take-up through the sap, are the best approach where they can be used.

On Vegetables

Malathion and *Diazinon* are the common choice. *Malathion* is less toxic. Repeat applications every 10-21 days, as needed. Complete coverage, including the underside of leaves, is essential for control. Both are toxic to bees pollinating the crops. When a crop is in bloom, apply *Malathion* only in the late evening when bees are not active. Do not use *Diazinon* on or near blooming crops.

Rotenone and *Pyrethrin* organic insecticides have a low toxicity to bees and are fair on aphids.

Cygon and *Di-Syston* systemic insecticide are excellent but have limited use on vegetables.

See the section of specific vegetables for insecticides to use on specific crops.

On Fruit Trees

Dormant sprays are very helpful in reducing overwintering egg populations.

Summer populations are best controlled by the home gardener with *Zolone*, *Diazinon* or *Malathion*.

On Flowers, Shrubs and Trees

Common insecticides as used on vegetables may be used, but here systemic insecticides are greatly superior. *Orthene* and *Cygon* give excellent control and can be used on most flowers, trees and shrubs. Both are highly toxic to bees and should never be used on or near blooming crops attracting bees. *Di-Syston,* applied to the soils, is common on some ornamentals, particularly roses.

CATERPILLARS
LOOPERS, CUTWORMS AND LEAFROLLERS

Caterpillars are the larvae of butterflies and moths. They may be smooth, hairy or decorated with spines, and may be drab in appearance or highly colorful. They are rounded, worm-like, and have thirteen segments behind the head. Caterpillars have three pairs of jointed legs with a claw-like toe on the first three body segments after the head. They also have two to five pairs of leg-like sucker feet, called prolegs, found along their body. Tiny hooks on the tips of the prolegs help the caterpillar hold onto leaves and stems. (Some beetle larvae, called grubs, may look similar, but beetle grubs do not have the prolegs.)

Caterpillars form pupa, called cocoons, at the completion of this stage of life. They then emerge from the cocoon as an adult butterfly or moth. The cycle continues as the adult lays eggs.

Adults vary greatly in appearance. For example, the adult of the imported cabbageworm is the common white butterfly seen flitting around the cabbage and broccoli patch. The adults of cutworms and armyworms are drab-colored, night-flying moths with wing spreads of up to 1 1/2 inches. They are attracted to lights. On the other hand the Parsleyworm adult is the beautiful Black Swallowtail Butterfly.

Various types of caterpillars are often grouped according to feeding habits or appearance. For example, *Loopers* refers to those who walk in a looping or measuring-worm style. *Leafrollers* and *Leaf-tiers* will roll up or tie up their leaves with silk. *Tent caterpillars* build silken tents around branches in which to live. *Case bearers* or *Bagworms* carry around their silk and dirt homes, much like a snail. *Hornworms* have a distinct horn on the back end. *Cutworms* refer to those caterpillars who feed by cutting off the plant. *Armyworms* refers to caterpillars which migrate in masses across a garden or field, eating everything as they move, like an army.

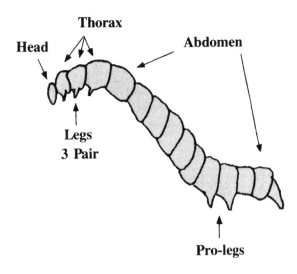

Caterpillars, the larvae of butterflies and moths, have three pairs of legs on the thorax (on the first three body segments past the head) and two to five pairs of leg-like sucker feet called prolegs. Caterpillar-like larvae of other insects lack the prolegs.

The names given to caterpillars are generally descriptive of their appearance or diet. The more common caterpillar pests in the garden include the following:

Cabbage Loopers are common green loopers with thin white stripes. They feed primarily on broccoli, Brussels sprouts, cabbage, cauliflower, collards, horseradish, kale, kohlrabi, mustard, radish and turnips. Beets, celery, lettuce, parsley, peas, potatoes, spinach, tomatoes, carnations, chrysanthemums, geraniums and other flowers are also attacked. They spend the winter as cocoons attached to plant debris.

Caterpillars are often named for their appearance or feeding habit. "Loopers" refers to those who walk in a measuring worm or looping fashion. (Photos: U.S.D.A. Extension Service)

Celery Loopers are light green with dark stripes. They feed on celery, beets, lettuce and other succulent plants and weeds.

Cutworms are typically hairless (a few small hairs are present but are rarely noticed) and may reach a length of 1 1/2 inches when fully grown. They are mottled, or striped in dull grays, browns, and greens. Cutworms hide in the soil in the day, feeding at night. Species common to the Intermountain West include the Army Cutworm, Variegated Cutworm, Dingy Cutworm, Glassy Cutworm, Dark-sided Cutworm, along with others.

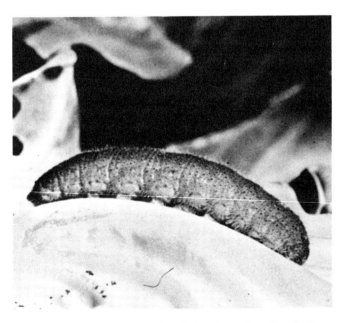

(Left) Cutworm chewing off corn seedling. (Right) Imported cabbage worm. (Photos: U.S.D.A. Extension Service)

Imported Cabbageworms are smooth green with alternating light and dark stripes. They feed on cabbage, cauliflower, broccoli, Brussels sprouts, kale, collards, kohlrabi, lettuce, mustard, radish, turnips, horseradish, nasturtiums, alyssums and others.

Tomato Fruitworms are green, brown or pinkish caterpillars with light stripes along their sides and back, and grow up to 1 3/4-inches long. They feed on fruit buds. Tomato fruit worms are known as the Corn Earworm when they feed on corn.

Hornworms are large green caterpillars with diagonal lines on their sides and a prominent horn on their rear end. They can grow up to four inches long. They have a voracious appetite for foliage and fruit of tomatoes, eggplant, and peppers. Their coloring gives them excellent camouflage, making them difficult to find. These pests can be hand picked (if you can find them).

Parsleyworms are the beautiful caterpillar of the Black Swallowtail Butterfly. They grow to two inches long, with black crossbands on each body segment. Two soft-forked orange horns are located just back of the head. The Parsleyworm's diet includes celery, carrots, dill, parsnips. etc.

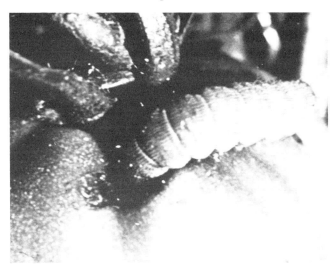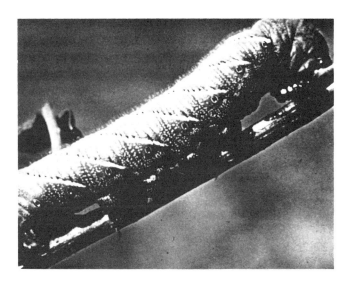

(Left) Tomato Fruitworm. (Right) the Hornworm's natural coloring provides excellent camouflage on tomato plants. (Photos: U.S.D.A. Extension Service)

Western Yellow Armyworms have smooth bodies and are velvety black with yellow stripes. They migrate in masses devouring alfalfa, tomatoes, rhubarb, melons, grapes, etc.

Zebra Caterpillars are very striking in appearance, being named for their black-and-white vertical stripes. Their lifestyle is similar to the cutworm's and armyworm's.

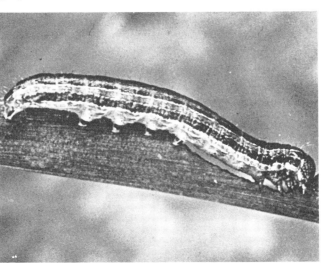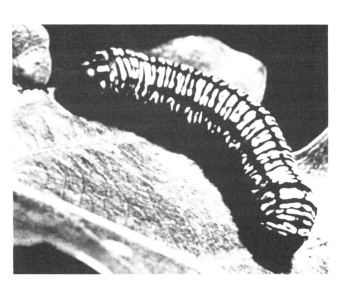

(Left) Typical Armyworms devour everything in their path as they migrate. (Right) The colorful Zebra Caterpillar. (Photos: U.S.D.A. Extension Service)

Butterflies and moths feed on nectar and generally do not damage plants. However their young, the caterpillar, have voracious appetites. Most feed on leaves, stems and fruits. Subterranean cutworms also feed on the plant crown and roots, just under the soil line.

Controlling Caterpillars

Good weed control and other sanitation practices to remove plant debris from the garden and immediate vicinity may reduce the attractiveness of the area to the egg-laying moths. Fall plowing of the garden will help destroy a portion of over-wintering larvae and pupa.

Since populations of many caterpillars can explode overnight, gardeners should keep an eye open for their attack. Leaves can be stripped in just a few days, and the pests may move on without being observed. A small population can be hand picked, but large populations generally require sprays to prevent crop losses.

The adults of many of the pests, like cutworms and imported cabbageworms, are night flying. They are attracted to lights and bug zappers. Placing a bug zapper too close to a garden will call in the adults from around the neighborhood and thus increase the problem in the garden.

A diseased caterpillar - Mother Nature uses insect diseases as a natural control on many insects. The bacteria *Bacillus thuringinensis* (Dipel, Thuricide) is a disease which man uses as an insecticide for the control of caterpillars. (Photo: U.S.D.A. Extension Service)

Leaf-feeding caterpillars are easy to control with the biological control agent *Bacillus thuringinensis (B.t.,* Dipel, Thuricide). This excellent insecticide is a bacterial disease of caterpillars and has the advantage of being non-toxic to other wildlife and humans. *B.t.* has a shorter shelf life than most sprays. It will hold its viability only for two years and should be protected from potential freezing and thawing.

On crops like broccoli, cabbage, and cauliflower, the sprays must be applied often to prevent the pests from penetrating the head or fruit. Reapplication is generally needed at 14-day intervals through the season.

Other common garden insecticides are also effective on most caterpillars. However *B.t.,* being less toxic, is strongly preferred.

Controlling Cutworms and Armyworms

Cutworms and armyworms are much more difficult to stop. They hide beneath clods and surface debris during the day and climb up the plant in the evening or on cloudy days to feed on the foliage, flowers, and developing fruit. A severe infestation can wipe a crop out in a few nights. A patch of cabbage and broccoli, or a row of beans or corn, can be cut off as effectively as if a lawn mower got out of control!

Some cutworms feed predominately on the plant's crown and underground stems, often cutting small plants off at or below ground level. These cutworms move up and down in the soil in response to soil moisture. They are usually found around the moisture line in the soil. If the top 1/2 inch of soil is dry, the larvae will be found an inch or so deeper. If the soil is saturated, the larvae will be at or on the surface. Damage usually occurs early in the season when plants are small. A heavy infestation may destroy a major portion of a crop. Late plantings often escape severe injury.

Individual plants may be protected from cutworms by placing paper or plastic collars around their bases, but some damage may still occur where cutworms crawl over or under the collars. The collar should extend 1-2 inches into the soil.

Where infestation appears light, damage may be minimized by digging around plants to locate and destroy individual cutworms. Be careful not to damage the young plant's roots in the process! This approach is a hit-and-miss method and results may be unsatisfactory.

Insecticide sprays provide fair control if they are applied when the cutworms are small and feeding above ground. Sprays applied after the cutworms enter the soils may still provide some control if the larvae are not too deep. To maximize results, water first to bring the pests to the surface, and spray in the evening.

A good population of subterranean cutworms is rather difficult to control with sprays. Here soil application of a granular Diazinon insecticide may give some help. Rake it into the top few inches of soil and water thoroughly. Gardeners who have a history of cutworm damage should apply the Diazinon Granules at planting time.

EARWIGS

The common European Earwig is easy to identify with its long (up to 1/4-inch) forcep-like cerci or pinchers at the end of its abdomen. The pincers are relatively straight in the female, and longer and curved in the male. Earwigs are dark reddish-brown, elongated, and up to 1-inch long. They do not bite; but if handled will attempt to inflict a painful pinch. Adults have two pairs of small wings but rarely fly. The membranous hind wings fold crosswise under the leathery front wings.

Adults spend the winter in protected places around the garden. The smooth, white, oval eggs are laid in batches in protected areas in the soil or under litter. The female watches over the eggs and very young. The young resemble small adults.

Earwigs are nocturnal. They hide in any convenient place during the day and come out to feed at night. They feed primarily on decaying materials, but will also attack leaves, blossoms, fruits, vegetables and insects. Some experts have suggested that their attacks on corn, peaches and apricots may include a successful dinner on other insects like corn earworms or twig borers. Their presence is generally more disconcerting than their feeding damage.

Controlling Earwigs

Earwig populations can be reduced by good yard and garden sanitation, removing surface debris which provides their shelter. Most common garden insecticides are effective on earwigs. *Dursban* is a good choice for spraying around non-edibles, and *Malathion* for use on vegetables.

 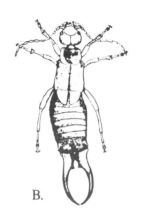 

(Left) European Earwigs: A. Female; B. male. (Right) grasshoppers eat irregular-shaped holes in leaves. (Photos: U.S.D.A. Extension Service)

GRASSHOPPERS

If you live adjacent to unplowed lands such as vacant lots, road rights-of-way, foothills, etc., you are well aware of the plague of grasshoppers. While no easy answer to grasshopper control exists, here are a few suggestions which may help in bad grasshopper years.

Grasshoppers live through the winter as eggs laid in the soils. The best grasshopper control method is to destroy the eggs by plowing or cultivating the soil in the late fall or early spring. The main grasshopper problems develop, however, as migrations occur from those lands which are not plowed or cultivated.

Spraying the breeding grounds (those uncultivated, weedy areas) is effective for grasshopper control. These areas should be sprayed in late spring as the young grasshoppers begin to hatch. This would be practical for localized infestation areas such as vacant lots. Where this is not practical, a border spray will be helpful.

Grasshoppers take a bite or two then fly or jump a few feet, take another couple of bites and move again. It is a cycle of eat and run, eat and run. As grasshoppers move into a garden adjoined by a weed area they typically make several stops along the way on the tall weeds.

Border spraying may prove very successful in such situations. Simply spray a band, typically 10-feet wide, around the garden or yard to be protected. If the migration is from one direction, it would be necessary to treat only that side. Border sprays need to be applied on plant materials where grasshoppers stop; spraying a driveway or street is not effective.

Blanket sprays over the entire yard are not very effective in grasshopper control. The grasshoppers will do considerable damage before the pesticide terminates them. And this heavy use of an insecticide is environmentally unsound.

Insecticide treatment for grasshoppers should begin as soon as the pests are observed. Young grasshoppers are much more sensitive to sprays than the old. Several insecticides are somewhat effective on grasshoppers; *Dursban* is the first choice.

Dursban is especially the product of choice for border spraying. The label indicates that treatments last 2-4 weeks, but many last even longer. *Dursban* is not cleared for use on fruits and vegetables, so be careful not to spray the vegetables, just around them. When using *Dursban* around blooming plants, apply it only in the late evening when bees are not active.

Malathion is a good choice where fruits or vegetables must be sprayed. It is not as effective as *Dursban*, and likely will need reapplication every 3-7 days under heavy grasshopper pressure. When using *Malathion* around blooming plants, spray only in the late evening when bees are not active.

Sevin (carbaryl) is sometimes used on range land for grasshopper control but it is a poor choice for the home gardener. It is far less effective on grasshoppers than *Dursban* or *Malathion*. It is ineffective on older more mature grasshoppers. However, the environmental hazards are the biggest objection. Blanket sprays of carbaryl should be avoided due to its extreme toxicity to bees. Bees will also actively gather *Sevin* dust as pollen, thus contaminating the beehive. Carbaryl will also aggravate problems with spider mites.

The grasshopper spore, *Nosema locustae*, sounds great in theory. This natural disease of grasshoppers has been effective in reducing populations on large tracks of range land. In the home garden, where small areas are treated in reaction to a large moving pest population, the bacteria can not keep up. A simple reduction in the grasshopper population will not prevent major crop losses in a garden setting.

LEAFHOPPERS

Leafhopper adults are yellowish green, slender, wedge-shaped, and up to 1/8-inch long. Two pairs of wings are held in a roof-like position when at rest. These active bugs fly quickly when disturbed. Large eyes and hair-like antennae dominate their triangle-shaped heads. The young, called nymphs, resemble adults but are smaller, and they crawl sideways like crabs. Leafhoppers spend the winter as adults hiding in weed patches, particularly weeds in the mustard family.

Leafhoppers feed on plant foliage by piercing the leaf and sucking the sap. When populations are heavy, a whitening of the foliage known as "hopper burn" may occur. Under heavy populations, leaves may become sticky, crinkled and curled, and the plants lose vigor. The most serious damage caused by their feeding is the spread of virus diseases.

Several species of leafhoppers are common in the Intermountain West. The most talked about leafhopper is the Beet Leafhopper. This pest lives on the native foliage of the arid west, moving into gardens in great swarms as the foothills and deserts dry in the early summer. Curly Top Virus, common to tomatoes, is spread by the beet leafhopper.

Leafhoppers can be found on a wide host of plants including alfalfa, apples, beans, beets, cherries, eggplant, dahlia, grapes, legumes, peaches, potatoes, rhubarb, roses, tomatoes and a long list of common weeds.

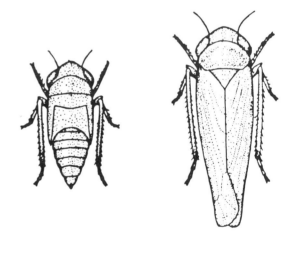

Leafhoppers, young (left) and adult (right) (Photos: University of Idaho Extension Service)

Controlling Leafhoppers

Control local weed patches which harbor the pest. Watch for migrations in the spring through early summer as the native open areas dry down. Sprays are not generally needed for a light population. When populations become heavy, sprays of *Malathion, Diazinon, Cygon, Methoxychlor, Pyrethrin* or *Sevin* are helpful.

SLUGS AND SNAILS

Slug and snails are common and annoying pests in yards and gardens. The term slug refers to those without shells, the term snails refers to those with shells. Control is the same on both.

Slugs range in size from one-forth inch to several inches in length, depending upon the species. They vary in color from whitish yellow, through various shades of gray to black. Usually they are more or less mottled or marked with darker shades of color. Their mouth is a rasping type and they scrape plants as they feed. They move on a moisture film, leaving a slime trail behind.

Slugs and snails feed in the evening or on cloudy days and remain hidden on hot, sunny days. They will feed on virtually any organic materials they can ingest, preferring young seedlings and succulent fruits. Damage consists of large, irregular eaten areas.

Slugs and snails are common everywhere but get out of control when their populations are allowed to reproduce without restraint. Carefully watch for their build-up in perennial beds, groundcovers and strawberries where they have continual cover.

Preventative Measures

Slugs and snails are very susceptible to desiccation (drying) and require a moist, shady place to live. Cultural practices which promote a dry, sunny environment will help discourage them.

Thinning out plants in order to open the canopy and dry the soil surface will deter slugs and snails to a great extent. In strawberries, for example, slugs are very common because the beds are often over-crowded with plants. Thinning strawberries to 6-inches apart will not only improve crop production but help control slugs and snails.

Avoid frequent waterings. Gardens should receive a heavy, infrequent irrigation, allowing the soil surface to dry between waterings.

Keep all loose boards, bricks, stones, trash piles, and other debris picked up, to remove their hiding places.

Slug and snail control should be directed towards preventing large populations from developing. This means early and consistent control of the slug population to prevent egg laying. Special care should be taken to control slugs and snails during cool, wet periods of the spring and fall. The greatest egg-laying activities occur at this time. Egg clusters should be destroyed when found. Eggs look like white, 1/8-inch pearls in clusters and are found wherever slugs and snails hide.

Commercial Baits

Commercially prepared baits containing *Metaldehyde* or *Measurol* are effective in reducing slugs and snails. *Metaldehyde* materials can be used around fruits and vegetables as long as they do not contact the edible portions of the crop. *Measurol* is only for use around non-edible plants. Place the bait out of access to pets, birds, and other wildlife.

Metaldehyde and *Measurol* are available in several brand names of granular and pellet-type baits. They can be scattered under plants or placed in bait stations. They are best applied in the evening when the soil is slightly damp. These baits need to be slightly moist to be effective, but they dissipate quickly when water logged. Carefully place the baits under plants, away from birds and pets which may be attracted to the bait. Spray formulations are also available.

The best commercial material is the metaldehyde in a paste formulation, commonly called *Deadline* and *Snail Line*. This paste material squeezes out like a gray toothpaste. Just put drops here and there on the ground under the plants being attacked. Rain and sprinklers do not decrease its effectiveness as with the dry baits. It is less attractive to pets and birds, not being a toy-like pellet.

If you prefer the pellet type, the new *Deadline Bullet* is excellent. This water-resistant bait lasts much longer than the older type bran pellet.

Other products, like *Sevin* (carbaryl), are sometimes added to provide some control of other pests like sowbugs and pillbugs. Insecticides alone are ineffective on slugs and snails.

Bait Stations

Since baits attract slugs and snails from several feet away, the use of bait stations placed in strategic spots is efficient and effective. Stations help protect pets, birds and other non-target animals which are attracted to the exposed bait. Baits will also last longer when not exposed to rain, irrigation water and drying sun.

Small piles of bait covered with a slightly propped-up board is the simplest bait station. The area remains somewhat moist so snails and slugs tend to congregate there anyway.

Milk cartons with "doorways" may be laid on their sides. Bait placed inside the carton is accessible but protected from rain or irrigation and does not touch the soil.

Plastic food containers like cottage cheese and yogurt cartons which have tight-fitting lids may be converted to a more elaborate bait station. They are even more difficult for non-target species to obtain access into. To lure the slugs or snails into the station, you can use commercial or home-made baits. Check the trap frequently to remove dead slugs and replenish the bait.

Commercial baits can be slightly moistened with water, apple juice or orange juice.

The reservoir may be filled with beer or yeast water. The pest is attracted, falls into the liquid and drowns. Removal of the carcasses is necessary to keep attracting additional clients.

The bait station may be used anywhere slugs and snails are active because the container keeps the bait from contacting the soil or plants. Logical locations are around the garden perimeter to intercept those migrating from ground-covers, perennials or other favorable habitats. Place the stations where the most slug activity occurs.

Easy-to-Make Bait Station

Milk Carton bait station

Cut a 1/2" to 1" slot on two sides of a container. Bury it so the slots are level with the soil.

Make a 1/2" to 34" hole near the center of the lid. Bury the container so the lid is at soil level.

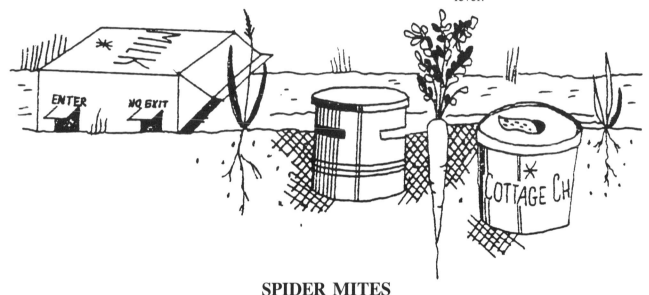

SPIDER MITES

Spider mites or red spiders are the general names used to describe several diverse species of plant-feeding mites. They are not insects nor spiders, though related. The "spider" in the common name refers to their ability to produce a very fine silk webbing on their host plants.

The most common species found in gardens is the two-spotted spider mite. The female adult is 1/60-inch long, with the males being shorter and more slender. They have a head and one main body segment (compared to the three-part body of insects). Mites have four pairs of legs. They can be colored red, reddish yellow, yellow, greenish or blackish, depending on the season. During the summer they are usually yellowish with an area of tiny red spots on each side of the body.

Their eggs are spherical, translucent, straw-colored, and hatch in 3-5 days. The newly hatched mites have only six legs, but they acquire an additional pair at their first molt. Their life cycle can be completed within 10 days. When

the summer temperatures reach into the high nineties, mite populations explode by the thousands daily. Winter is spent as immature adults in sheltered areas like the cracks of tree bark and in plant debris.

Mites prefer to feed on the underside of the leaves along the veins. Spider mites feed by piercing the leaf surface and sucking up plant fluids, removing the chlorophyll in the process. Individual feeding sites appear as pin-point sized yellow or white spots. The spots merge together giving the infested area a light colored, dusty bronze appearance. As the damage spreads, the leaf eventually dries up and turns brown. Very, very fine webbing may coat the plant. Infected plants turn off-color and lose vigor due to the loss of photosynthetic surface. A heavy infestation will kill plants.

Spider mites have a wide range of host plants, depending on the species. Beans, cantaloupes, celery, corn, cucumbers, eggplants, melons, parsnips, peppers, potatoes, pumpkins and squash are vegetables commonly attacked by mites. All kinds of fruit are subject to mite attacks. A very common site for mite attacks is on marigolds. Varieties like the "Crush" marigold are hypersensitive, while other varieties like the "Inca" and "Discovery" marigold are resistant. Asters, begonias, chrysanthemums, delphiniums, fuchsias, glads, geraniums, hollyhocks, junipers, marigolds, phlox, pines, snapdragons, spruces, tulips and zinnias are common ornamentals with mite problems. Most house plants are subject to attack. And the list could go on.

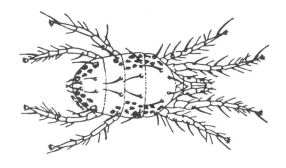

(Left) Two spotted Spider Mites (Drawing: University of Idaho Extension Service) (Right) Spider mites are too small to be noticeable with the naked eye, but their very fine webbing is noticeable. (Photo: U.S.D.A. Extension Service)

Controlling Spider Mites

Whenever you see a plant looking a little speckled, bronzed and dusty, you should suspect mites. Mites are too small to be visible to the naked eye, but you can easily check for them if you have a small hand lens or magnifying glass. You'll need about a 10-power lens. Check on the underside of the leaf along the veins for mite activity, webbing, eggs and shed skins.

If you don't have a lens, you may be able to find activity by placing a white sheet of paper under the leaf suspected of harboring mites. Tap the leaf or branch sharply, then withdraw the paper and turn it on edge to discard any dirt and debris. Any live mites will cling to the paper and appear as small grains of "moving dust."

Mites are generally favored by hot, dry dusty conditions. You typically do not see mite problems until it turns hot, and then they explode! They are so common that you should routinely keep an eye open for them in July and August.

The primary control of mites is through the protection of mite predators. The most important predators of plant-feeding mites are mite-feeding mites. The mite-feeding mites are sensitive to common insecticides, so avoid all unnecessary use of insecticides. Also *do not* use the insecticide *Sevin* (carbaryl) on mite-sensitive plants. *Sevin* is not only very toxic to mite predators, but also causes a localized plant-feeding mite population to spread rapidly.

Whenever there are signs of mite problems, it indicates that the predators cannot keep up, and you must move quickly to prevent a major outbreak. Many gardeners don't notice the impending problem until a major outbreak has occurred, and at that point they have a difficult time stopping the outbreak.

Sprays must be directed at the underside of leaves and applied with high volumes of water to assure contact with the mites. Repeat spraying at 7- to 14-day intervals to catch newly hatched eggs. Rotate the insecticides used to help prevent the mites from becoming resistant to the spray.

There aren't any sprays in the home garden trade which are excellent for mite control. These little pests reproduce so fast that their resistance to miticides develops rapidly. The newer, more effective miticides are either not registered for use on most home garden crops, are not registered for homeowner use, or are not available in small packages.

The home garden miticides for use on vegetables and fruits include the following:

Diazinon. To protect bees, do not apply when crops are in bloom.

Malathion. When crops are in bloom, apply only in the late evening when bees are not active.

Cygon. This systemic insecticide is registered for use on some vegetables (see section on the specific vegetable).

To protect bees, do not apply when crops are in bloom. Protective clothing is needed for application.

On non-edible crops, *Orthene, Isotox,* and *Cygon* systemic insecticides are currently providing the best approach to mite control. Alternate between them. To protect pollinating bees, do not apply *Orthene, Isotox,* or *Cygon* to crops in bloom. *Kelthane,* an old standard miticide, generally gives disappointing control.

THRIPS

The yellow or brown adults have two pairs of feather-type wings. They are very active but hard to see, being only 1/25-inch long. The young look like small adults, but are white and wingless.

Thrips feed on blossoms and on the underside of lower leaves. They feed by rasping and puncturing the cells on the plant surface, causing a "silvering" of a portion of the lower surface. Severely injured leaves dry prematurely; buds and fruit may become scarred or deformed; and plants may be stunted.

Controlling Thrips

Thrips show up as the native weed hosts begin to dry and the pests move to fresh green materials. While the infestations vary from season to season, a light population generally does not merit chemical control.

They are difficult to control with any insecticide; the best choices would be *Malathion, Diazinon,* or *Cygon*. Complete coverage, including the underside of lower leaves, will be necessary. Make two or three applications at 7-14 day intervals.

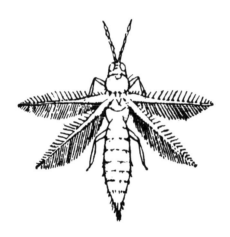 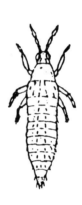

The winged adult thrip (left) and young (right) (Pictures: University of Idaho Extension Service)

9
Insect and Disease Problems of Vegetables

ASPARAGUS

Pollination: flowers on the asparagus fern are insect pollinated. When applying insecticides, use caution to protect the pollinating bees when plants are in bloom.

Insecticides to Use on Asparagus

Malathion (1 day from application to harvest) When asparagus fern is in bloom; spray only late evening, when bees are not active.

Methoxychlor (3 days from application to harvest) When asparagus fern is in bloom; apply only late evening to early morning when bees are not active.

Pyrethrin (0 days from application to harvest) Organic insecticide.

Rotenone (1 day from application to harvest) Organic insecticide.

Sevin (1 day from application to harvest) Good control on beetles, but to protect bees, do not apply when asparagus is in bloom.

NOTE: *Do not* use *Diazinon* on asparagus.

Insects of Asparagus

Asparagus Beetles, *Crioceris spp.* The adults are metallic-blue-to-black beetles with red to yellow markings, 1/4-inch long. They spend the winter as adults, hiding in protective debris around the garden. Eggs laid on asparagus spears look like shiny black specks. The eggs hatch in about a week into olive green to dark gray, 1/2-inch-long soft larvae or grubs. Grubs drop to the soil to pupate. The life cycle takes 3-8 weeks, with two or more generations per season.

Adults and grubs eat foliage, leaving the shoots misfigured. Heavy populations can defoliate plants. Damage is most severe in the spring.

Control: Lady beetles and predaceous plant bugs feed on this pest. Frequent cutting will often give adequate control. When the beetle population is heavy, insecticides such as *Rotenone, Malathion, Sevin* or *Pyrethrin* may be helpful.

Flea Beetles—see Potatoes - Flea Beetles.

Diseases of Asparagus

Frost Injury

Symptoms: Twisting and drying of tender spears, caused by spring frost and cold weather. Common in cool springs.
Control: none.

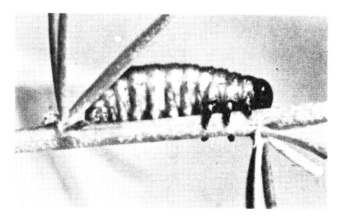

Asparagus Beetle adult (left) and larva (right) (Photo: U.S.D.A. Extension Service)

BEANS

Pollination: while insect pollination is not required for bean production, the blossoms are often visited by pollen-collecting insects. When applying insecticides, use caution to protect these insect friends.

Insecticides for Use on Beans

Bacillus thuringiensis (Dipel, Thuricide) (0 days from application to harvest) An excellent biological control agent for use on caterpillars.

Cygon (0 days from application to harvest) To protect bees, do not apply when crop is in bloom. This is a good systemic insecticide, but its use is limited by protective clothing needed for application. Use on beans in hot weather can cause some minor leaf damage.

Diazinon (7 days from application to harvest) To protect bees, do not apply when crop is in bloom.

Di-Syston (60 days from application to harvest) This is an excellent systemic insecticide giving long-term pest control. Use is limited to applications at planting only. Wear protective gloves when applying.

Malathion (1 day from application to harvest) When crop is in bloom, apply only in late evening when bees are not active.

Methoxychlor (3 days from application to harvest) When crop is in bloom, apply only from late evening to early morning when bees are not active.

Pyrethrin (0 days from application to harvest) Organic insecticide with a very short control period.

Rotenone (1 day from application to harvest) Organic insecticide with quick knockdown power but a short control residue.

Sevin (0 days from application to harvest) To protect bees, do not apply to crops in bloom. Not recommended for use on beans due to mite build-up following use.

Thiodan (3 days from application to harvest) When crop is in bloom, apply only from late evening to early morning when bees are not active.

Insects of Beans

Aphids—see Aphids.
Cutworms—see Caterpillars, Cutworms.
Flea Beetles—see Potatoes - Flea Beetles.
Leafhoppers—see Leafhoppers.
Lygus Bugs. These stink-bug-type pests are green to dark brown, slender, and up to 1/4-inch long. They spend the winter in weed patches.

Their feeding may kill young bean plants or the terminal portion of older plants. Their attacks on the blossoms cause bud drop. Their attacks on the forming bean pod causes small, malformed "cat-faced" beans.

Control: Control weed patches. Where necessary, common garden spray will be helpful.

Mexican Bean Beetles, *Epilachna varivestis.* Adults are 1/3-inch long, copper-colored, oval ladybugs with 16 black spots arranged in three rows across the body. Orange-yellow eggs are laid in clusters on the leaf underside. The soft-bodied larvae or grub is orange-yellow, fuzzy or spiny, up to 1/3-inch long. Spiny, orangish pupa are also found attached to leaf undersides. Two generations can occur each season. The adults spend the winter under the protective covering of leaves and other debris.

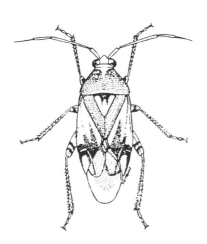 

(Left) Lygus Bug (Picture: University of Idaho Extension Service) (Right) Mexican Bean Beetles; pupa, adult, eggs, and larvae (Photo: U.S.D.A. Extension Service)

The feeding of adults and larvae skeletonizes the leaves, leaving only main veins. Pods may also be damaged. This pest will be a serious problem some years and not at all other seasons.

Control: Early plantings are very prone to attack. Late plantings isolated from other beans seem less bothered. Hand removal is often listed as an organic control but with a high population, this may be rather impractical.

This pest is controllable where sprays keep the population down, but difficult to stop when the population gets high. Spray when the pests first appear, repeating at 10-14 day intervals, as needed. Complete coverage, including underside of leaves, is essential for control. Insecticides for the Mexican Bean Beetle include the following:

Rotenone (organic) is good but frequent reapplication is required due to its short residue.

Malathion is good with complete coverage (evening application only).

Cygon is great, but should not be used during blossoming.

Diazinon is good, but again, should not be used during blossoming.

Sevin is great but is not recommended due to bee kill and mite build-up following use.

Di-Syston is great, but must be applied at planting time.

Pyrethrin (organic) is okay, requiring very frequent repeat application.

Gardeners who have a yearly problem with bean beetles may find *Di-Syston* applied at planting a good way to control early season populations. The chemical will run out just before the beans are ready for the first picking. During blooming you may have good success with *malathion* and/or *rotenone*.

Seed Corn Maggot— see Corn - Seed Corn Maggot.

Spider Mites—See Spider Mites (common pest of beans).

Western Bean Cutworm, *Loxagrotis albicosta.* The adult moth, which is active only at night, has a body about 3/4-inch long and a wing span of 1 1/2-inches. The forewings are rich brown with a very light narrow band along the front margin. The hind wings are light tan shading to darker brown on the outer margin. Adults emerge from early July to mid August and live from 7 to 9 days. Eggs are laid en masse on leaves.

Their caterpillar is one of the climbing cutworms, feeding upon the plant at night and hiding in the soil around the plant in the daytime. It is pinkish brown, about 1 1/2-inches long, and 1/4-inch in diameter when mature. Watch for the larvae from late July through September. As cool weather approaches, the larvae enters the soil to spend the winter.

On beans the newly hatched caterpillars feed on leaves, buds and blossoms. When half grown, they begin to feed

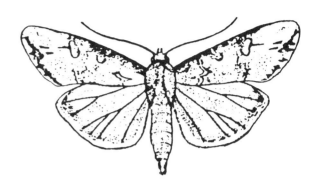

Western Bean Cutworm larva and adult moth. (Picture: University of Idaho Extension Service)

on beans pods and developing seeds. They feed mostly at night and spend the day in the soil around the plant.

In corn the larvae bore directly through the side of the corn husk and feed on the corn ear. They remain inside their tunnels under the husk in the day.

Control: This common pest is more serious on sandy soils than on heavier clays. It is typically serious one year and not other years. Watch for the young cutworm from mid July to mid August. A blacklight bug trap will catch the adult moths.

The biological spray *Bacillus thuringinensis* should do a good job on controlling this pest. *Sevin* is also effective, but is not recommended due to complications with bee kill and spider mite build-up.

Researchers have found that using a blacklight too near the garden can greatly increase the damage from this pest. While blacklights may be a helpful tool to determine a moth's flight, they attract moths into the garden area from the surrounding neighborhoods.

Thrips—see Thrips.

Bean Diseases

Damping Off.

Pathogen: Pythium spp., fungus.

Symptoms: Seeds decay in the soil. Young plants collapse at the soil line, fall over and die. The fungi lives in soil.

Control: Most gardeners have experienced damping off on cool wet springs. Allow soil to warm and dry before planting. Use fungicide-treated seed (*Captan, Thiram* or *Terrachlor*).

Dampening off on beans. Plants are killed at soil level. (Photos: U.S.D.A. Extension Service)

Common Bean Mosaic Virus.
Pathogen: Mosaic Virus.
Symptoms: Leaves have a yellow-green mottling, may be cupped downward or deformed, and may have some veinal necrosis (die back along leaf veins). Early infections result in dwarfed and spindly plants.
Control: This common disease has no cure for infected plants. Remove the infected plants to retard the spread of the disease. The virus is carried by aphids, movement of workers among the beans plants, and by infected seed. Some varieties have some resistance.

Fusarium Stem and Root Rot.
Pathogen: Fusarium spp., fungus.
Symptoms: Plants become stunted, leaves turn yellow and may drop early. The main root may discolor to red and then turn black and begin to rot. The secondary roots are killed.
Control: The fungus of this common disease lives in the soil. Practice crop rotation (4-year) where possible.

Plant in well drained soils and avoid over-irrigation. *Benomyl* sprays may help suppress this disease, but the cost may not justify the treatment.

Sclerotinia White Mold.
Pathogen: Sclerotina sclerotiorum fungus.
Symptoms: Dark water-soaked spots appear on leaves or stems, usually beginning near ground level. White, matted, cotton-like fungal growth develops on the stems, leaves or pods. Black sclerotia (fruiting body of the fungus) appear on the surface and inside stems. They look like rose thorns, 1/8- to 1/3-inch long. Plants wilt and die.
Control: When this disease occasionally hits it can quickly destroy the crop. Watch for it in cool damp weather and when the plants develop a solid canopy. The fungus lives in the soil, so do not till in nor compost diseased plants. Practice crop rotation when practical. Increase plant spacing to improve air circulation. When the disease gets started, *Benomyl* or *Ziram* sprays may be helpful.

BEETS & SWISS CHARD

Insecticides for Use on Beets and Chard
Bacillus thuringinensis (Dipel, Thuricide) (0 days from application to harvest) a biological control agent for caterpillars.
Diazinon (beets: 14 days from application to harvest) (chard: 12 days from application to harvest)
Malathion (7 days from application to harvest)
Methoxychlor (beets: 14 days from application to harvest on tops, 7 days on roots)
Rotenone (1 day from application to harvest) An organic insecticide.
Sevin (14 days from application to harvest for leaves; 3 days on beet roots)

Insects of Beets and Chard
Aphids—see Aphids.
Beet Leafhopper—see Tomatoes - Beet Leafhopper.

Cutworms—see Caterpillars - Cutworms.
Slugs—see Slugs.
Leaf Minor—see Spinach - Leaf Minor.
Wireworms—see Potatoes - Wireworms.

Diseases of Beets and Chard
Powdery Mildew.
Pathogen: Erysiphe sp., fungus.
Symptoms: White powdery patches on leaves and stems; may coalesce to cover entire leaf surface. Leaves turn chlorotic (yellow) and necrotic (brown). The mildew feeds on the plant's sugars, greatly reducing the beets' quality.
Control: This problem is more common in fall plantings, and can be controlled by treating with *benomyl* fungicide when the symptoms first appear (21 days from application to harvest). Repeat at 14-day intervals as needed.

Curly Top Virus.
Pathogen: Curly Top Virus.
Symptoms: Leaves become chlorotic (yellowish), notably thickened, leathery and brittle. The vein color fades and the veins may swell. The tap root is covered with many fine, hairy rootlets. Gardeners in the Intermountain West will occasionally see this disease randomly along the beet row.

Control: There is no cure for infected plants. Remove the plants showing symptoms to suppress the virus spread. Control area weed patches which harbor the beet leafhopper, the insect which spreads the virus. Crops planted and harvested early often escape the leafhopper flights. The variety *Parma Globe* is resistant to CTV.

CARROTS

Insecticides for Use on Carrots

Diazinon (10 days from application to harvest)
Malathion (7 days from application to harvest)
Methoxychlor (7 days from application to harvest)
Rotenone (1 day from application to harvest) An organic insecticide.
Sevin (0 days from application to harvest)
Thiodan (7 days from application to harvest)

Insects of Carrots

Aphids—see Aphids.
Symphylans, *Scutigerella immaculata.* These non-insect relatives are white, fragile looking, have 12 pairs of legs on the adults (fewer legs on the young), and are up to 3/8-inch long. They are active pests, and keep their long antennae constantly twitching. They are found in moist soils that contain decaying plant materials, and are rarely seen on the surface of the soils, being repelled by light.

Symphylans eat numerous tiny holes or pits into the underground portions of the plants. They eat off tiny roots and root hairs. Roots of injured plants have a blunted appearance. They may attack soft fruits, like strawberries, laying on the soil.

They attack carrots, corn, cucumbers, lettuce, radishes, tomatoes, strawberries, asters, sweetpeas, snapdragons, and other plants.

Control: It is fortunate that this pest is not common because it is difficult to control. When it becomes a problem, *Diazinon* granules cultivated into the soil before planting will reduce the population.

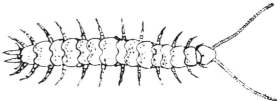

Garden Symphylan (Picture: U.S.D.A. Extension Service)

Wireworms—see Potatoes - Wireworms.

Diseases of Carrots

Soft Rot.
Pathogen: Erwinia carotovora bacteria
Symptoms: Soft, watery or slimy decay of roots; very common in storage. When the soil is soggy, carrot roots can rot in the ground. The carrot tops yellow and wilt as their roots rot.
Control: Bacteria survives in decaying refuse and enters roots through wounds. Where it occurs in the garden there is no cure. Over-watering will aggravate this problem. It is common in storage, resulting from harvest injury to the carrots and/or excessive moisture in storage.

CELERY

Insecticides for Use on Celery

Bacillus thuringiensis (Dipel, Thuricide) (0 days from application to harvest) A biological control insecticide for use on caterpillars.
Diazinon (10 days from application to harvest)
Malathion (7 days from application to harvest)
Pyrethrin (0 days from application to harvest) An organic insecticide with a short control period.
Thiodan (4 days from application to harvest)
Sevin (14 days from application to harvest)

Celery Insects

Aphids—see Aphids.
Cutworms—see Caterpillars - Cutworms.
Loopers and Caterpillars—see Caterpillars - Loopers.

Celery Diseases

Fusarium Yellows.
Pathogen: Fusarium oxysporum F. appi fungus.
Symptoms: Plants are off-colored and stunted, and their tissue is brittle and bitter. Infected seedlings may die; older plants will survive but become dwarfed. A longitudinal cut through the base of the stem will show yellow, reddish or black discoloration. This may extend into the roots and upward several inches.
Control: Control is aimed at prevention since there is no cure. Plant only healthy plants, moving the celery to a different garden area each year. The fungus lives in the soils, so diseased plants must be removed and destroyed, never composted nor plowed in. Some varieties have resistance.

COLE CROPS
Broccoli, Brussel Sprouts, Cabbage, Cauliflower, Kohlrabi

Insecticides for Use on Cole Crops

Bacillus thuringiensis (Dipel, Thuricide) (0 days from application to harvest) A great biological control agent for the control of caterpillars.

Chlorban (Dursban granules) (apply only at planting time) Excellent for root maggot control.

Cygon (7 days from application to harvest on broccoli and cauliflower, 3 days on cabbage) A systemic insecticide, excellent for aphids control. Protective clothing is needed for application.

Diazinon (5 days from application to harvest on broccoli and cauliflower, 7 days on cabbage and Brussel sprouts; do not use on kohlrabi)

Di-Syston (14 days from application to harvest on broccoli, 30 days on Brussel sprouts, 42 days on cabbage, 40 days on cauliflower) A systemic insecticide, excellent for aphid control, but watch that the long period from application to harvest does not interfere with harvest. Wear protective gloves when applying.

Malathion (3 days from application to harvest on broccoli, 7 days on cabbage, cauliflower, Brussel sprouts and kohlrabi)

Methoxychlor (14 days from application to harvest on broccoli and Brussel sprouts, 3 days on cabbage, 7 days on cauliflower and 1 day on kohlrabi)

Pyrethrin (0 days from application to harvest) An organic insecticide with a short control period.

Rotenone (1 day from application to harvest) An organic insecticide with a short control residue.

Sevin (3 days from application to harvest)

Thiodan (3 days from application to harvest on broccoli and cabbage, 14 days on cauliflower and Brussel sprouts, do not use on kohlrabi)

Cabbage Aphids (Photo: David Whiting)

Insects of Cole Crops

Aphids. Bluish green, oval-shaped aphids with a powdery, waxy covering are found in clusters on the underside of leaves. A common pest of cabbage, broccoli and cauliflower. See Aphids for more details.

Control: Spray as needed with *Malathion, Diazinon* or *Cygon.*

Cabbage Loopers, Cabbage Worms and Other Caterpillars. Several species of leaf-feeding caterpillars are very common on cole crops. They are generally green or grayish; markings vary with the species. The whitish butterflies frequently seen fluttering around the crop are the adults of many of these caterpillars. See Caterpillars for more details.

These caterpillars feed on the underside of leaves, producing ragged holes. The large loopers burrow into the cabbage heads, contaminating the crop.

Control: Care must be taken to control loopers and cabbage worms before they enter the cabbage heads. This is one pest most home gardeners must routinely treat for each season. Spray when the insects first appear, repeating every 10-14 days up to harvest. *Bacillus thuringiensis* (Dipel, Thuricide, *B.t.*) is an excellent biological control insecticide. It is not toxic to non-caterpillars. Complete coverage, including the underside of leaves, is essential for control. Insecticides for aphids can be added to this spray when needed. Other insecticides are effective but inferior to *B.t.*

Cabbage Root Maggot—see Radish - Cabbage Root Maggot.

Cutworms—see Caterpillars - Cutworms.

Flea Beetles—see Potatoes - Flea Beetles.

Slugs—see Slugs.

Diseases of Cole Crops

Bacterial Black Rot.

Pathogen: Xanthomonas campestris bacteria.

Symptoms: Leaves turn yellow (chlorotic), beginning at the margins and spreading inwards, creating a V-shaped area. Veins within the area turn black. Infection then enters the main stem, turning the inside black. With early infections, plants either die or are dwarfed. Late infections result in defoliation.

Control: The bacteria comes from infected seeds and infected soils. Dew, rain, and irrigation water spread the bacteria around, contaminating the soil. Remove infected plants and clean up all crop refuse. Avoid planting any cole crops, kale, mustard, radish, turnips and rutabaga in the infected garden area for 3 years.

Rhizoctonia Stem Rot.
Pathogen: Rhizoctonia sp. fungus.
Symptoms: Dry dark lesions develop on the stem. These may enlarge and girdle the plant, causing wilting and stunting. Other disease organisms may invade and cause a wet rot of stem or roots.
Control: Plant in a well-drained soil. Avoid heaping soil up around the stem.

CORN

Pollination: Corn is wind pollinated, but it is also heavily visited by bees collecting pollen. When applying insecticides during tasseling, use caution to protect the pollinating insects. Do *not* spray tassels with insecticides.

Insecticides for Use on Corn

Diazinon (5 days from application to harvest) To protect bees, do not apply when the crop is in tassel.

Di-Syston (40 days from application to harvest) Wear protective gloves when applying.

Malathion (5 days from application to harvest) When corn is in tassel, apply only in late evening when bees are not active.

Methoxychlor (7 days from application to harvest) When crop is in tassel, apply only in late evening, at night, or in early morning when bees are not active.

Pyrethrin (0 days from application to harvest) An organic insecticide with a short control period.

Rotenone (1 day from application to harvest) An organic insecticide, fair on aphids.

Sevin (0 days from application to harvest) To protect bees, do not apply when the crop is in tassel. *Not* recommended for use on corn due to potential bee kill and to mite build-up following use.

Insects of Corn

Aphids—see Aphids.

Corn Earworm, *Heliothis zea.*

These are the common worms found in corn ears at harvest time. The larvae or caterpillars are yellowish, green or brown, with light stripes along their sides and back. When fully grown they can be up to 2-inches long. Adult night-flying moths are generally a buff or tan color. It is easy to understand why these are such common pests, knowing that the adults are strong fliers and that the female can lay up to 3,000 eggs! On corn the eggs are generally laid on the silk, where the young caterpillars quickly feed down the silk and into the kernels and ear. These pests spend the winter as pupa (cocoons) in the top 2-6 inches of soil.

Primary damage occurs as they feed on the silk and kernels of the ears. Early feeding caterpillars attack newly unfolding leaves, causing a ragged appearance. They also attack tomatoes (called the tomato fruitworm), cotton (called the cotton bollworm) and beans, cabbage, broccoli, lettuce, geraniums, grapes, pumpkins, squash, strawberries, etc.

Control: This is a common but sporadic pest. Research staff at the University of Idaho's Parma Center found 2 years in 6 with only minor outbreaks, compared to 2 years in 6 of widespread heavy losses in untreated fields.

No treatment will control worms in the ears, so sprays must be carefully timed to control the larvae as they hatch on the silk, before the worms enter the ears. Start treatment when silking begins, repeating every 2-3 days until the silks turn brown. This usually involves four applications. When spraying, treat the silks only. Do *not* spray the tassels, which are visited by pollen-collecting bees.

The commonly used insecticides are *Diazinon* and *Sevin*. However, *Diazinon* and *Sevin* should not be used at this time due to potential bee kill! *Sevin* can also stimulate a spider mite problem. You can have good success with *Malathion* liquid, applied in the late evening when bees are not active.

Organic gardeners may try *Bacillus thuringinensis* (Dipel, Thuricide), an excellent biological control agent for caterpillars.

Corn Rootworm. Larvae are up to 1/2-inch long, white with brownish yellow heads. The adult beetles are 1/5-inch long, yellowish green.

Primary damage is from larvae feeding on roots, resulting in stunting, lodging and death of plants. This uncommon pest can cause extensive damage when it hits in a localized garden. Adults feed on silks and pollen and a host of other plants.

Control: In gardens where they have been a pest, apply *Diazinon, Sevin* or *Di-Syston* to the soil at planting.

Cutworms—see Caterpillars, cutworms.

Earwigs—see Earwigs.

Flea Beetles—see Potatoes - Flea Beetle.

Sap Beetles, *Nitidulids.*

Sap beetles are small, about 3/16-inch, oval, usually black and very active. They scatter rapidly over the ear when exposed to light. The white-to-cream-colored larvae are maggot-like (legless), up to 1/4-inch long, and also active. They move into the corn ears when the husk is loosened and feed on the kernels.

Control: Follow the spray program for corn earworm. (Note: *Bacillus thuringinensis*, a biological control agent, will not control this pest.)

Seed Corn Maggot, *Hylemya platura.*

The yellowish-white maggots (leg-less larva) are about 1/4-inch long, have successive raised rings of tissue marking the individual body segments, and pointed heads. The adults are a nondescript, grayish-brown fly with a slender body and long wings. They spend the winter as pupae in soil or manure, being attracted to soils rich in organic matter.

While there are several generations per year, the major injury occurs in the spring, when the maggots burrow into the developing seeds and plant stems. Under severe conditions, the emerging crop can be destroyed. Damage is more common in cool, wet springs and on soils with high organic matter. The maggot can transmit bacterial rots.

Beans, corn and peas are the most seriously injured crops. They can also cause occasional problems on beets, cabbage, cucumbers, melons, onions, peas, potatoes, radishes, spinach, turnips, gladioli and evergreen seedlings.

Control: Most gardeners have never seen this pest, but those who do often loose their entire crop. Avoid planting until soils have warmed sufficiently to allow for rapid germination and quick emergence of seeds. Shallow planting, which speeds germination, may be helpful where this is a problem. Gardeners who have had a serious problem with this pest can get some relief by adding *Diazinon* granules to the seed row at planting.

Spider Mites—see Spider Mites.

Symphylans—see Carrots - Symphylans.

Western Bean Cutworm—See Beans - Western Bean Cutworm.

The Corn Earworm. (Photo: U.S.D.A. Extension Service)

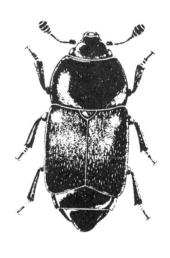

The Sap Beetle.

A.
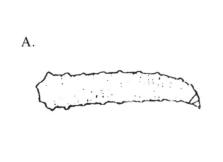

B.
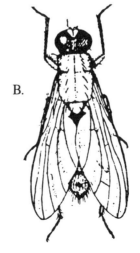

C.
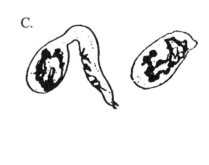

The Seed Corn Maggot: A, larva; B, adult; C, injured seed.

Corn Smut. (Photos U.S.D.A. and Pennsylvania State University Extension Service)

Diseases of Corn

Damping off.
Pathogen: Pythium spp. fungus.
Symptoms: Young seedlings suddenly wilt, fall over and die. Seeds fail to come up. This disease is very common in cool late springs.
Control: Avoid planting too early, when soils are cool and wet. Use fungicide-treated seeds (Captan or Thiram).
Smut.
Pathogen: Ustilago maydis fungus.

Symptoms: Large, irregularly shaped white galls or outgrowths form on stalks, ears, and tassels. Galls burst, releasing masses of black fungus spores, contaminating the soil.
Control: This disease is difficult to control. The fungus is spread through contaminated soils and manure, and infected seeds. Cutting off and destroying smut balls before they break open may reduce soil inoculation. Practice crop rotation where possible.

EGGPLANT

Pollination: Insect pollination is required for eggplant production. When applying insecticides, use caution to protect pollinating insects.

Insecticides for Use on Eggplant

Bacillus thuringinensis (Dipel, Thuricide) A biological control agent for caterpillars.
Malathion (3 days from application to harvest) When crop is in bloom; apply only in late evening when bees are not active.
Methoxychlor (7 days from application to harvest) When crop is in bloom; apply only from late evening to early morning when bees are not active.
Pyrethrin (0 days from application to harvest) An organic insecticide with a short control period.
Rotenone (1 day from application to harvest) An organic insecticide with a short control period.
Sevin (0 days from application to harvest) To protect bees, do not apply when crop is in bloom. Not recommended due to mite build-up following use.
Thiodan (1 day from application to harvest) When crop is in bloom; apply only from late evening to early morning when bees are not active.
NOTE: *Do not* use *Diazinon* on eggplant.

Insects of Eggplant

Aphids—see Aphids.
Flea Beetles—see Potatoes - Flea Beetles.
Leafhoppers—see Leafhoppers.

Stink Bug (Photo: U.S.D.A. Extension Service)

Stink Bugs. Adult stink bugs can be brown, green or black, and with or without markings, depending on the species. They are shield-shaped, up to 5/8-inch long and 1/3-inch wide. The young resemble the adults but are smaller. Stink bugs discharge a foul odor. Stink bugs spend the winter in protected spots around plant materials. Adults and young suck sap from plants. As a result, the plants are weakened and buds and young fruit are malformed.

Control: Control weed patches around the garden where the pest lives. If the population becomes threatening, spray with common insecticides like *Thiodan* or *Pyrethrin.*

Diseases of Eggplant

Blossom End Rot—see Tomatoes - Blossom End Rot.
Early Blight—see Tomatoes - Early Blight.
Verticillium Wilt—see Tomatoes - Verticillium.

LETTUCE

Insecticides for Use on Lettuce

Bacillus thuringiensis (Dipel, Thuricide) (0 days from application to harvest) A biological control agent for caterpillars.

Cygon (7 days on head lettuce, 14 days on leaf types) A systemic insecticide, excellent on leafhoppers. Use is limited by protective clothing needed for application.

Diazinon (10 days from application to harvest)
Malathion (7 days on head lettuce, 14 days on leaf types)
Methoxychlor (14 days from application to harvest)
Pyrethrin (0 days from application to harvest) An organic insecticide with a very short control period.

Rotenone (1 day from application to harvest) An organic insecticide.

Sevin (3 days on head lettuce, 14 days on leaf types)
Thiodan (14 days from application to harvest)

Insects of Lettuce

Aphids—see Aphids.
Caterpillars—see Caterpillars - Loopers.
Cutworms—see Caterpillars - Cutworms.
Leafhoppers—see Leafhoppers.
Slugs—see Slugs and Snails.

ONIONS

Insecticides for Use on Onions

Malathion (3 days from application to harvest)
Diazinon (10 days from application to harvest)
NOTE: *Do not* use *Sevin* or *Methoxychlor* on onions.

Insects of Onions

Cutworms—see Caterpillars - Cutworms.
Onion Root Maggot. These white leg-less maggots grow up to 1/3-inch long. The large winged, adult flys are brown or gray, 1/4-inch long, with a humpbacked appearance. The pests spend the winter as brown pupua in the soil or in cull onions. The maggots burrow into the onion bulbs, destroying the crop. The damage is more serious in wet years.

Control: Destroy cull onions immediately after harvest. Where needed, the foliage can be sprayed with *malathion* or *diazinon* when the flies first appear. Watch for them about the time forsythia blooms. *Diazinon* granules, applied to the soil at planting time, also are effective.

Thrips—see Thrips.

Diseases of Onions

Neck Rot.
Pathogen: Botrytis allii fungus.
Symptoms: This is the common rot in onion storage. Water-soaked spots appear on the neck area, turning yellow. Gray mold grows between the bulb scales, and the bulb deteriorates. Symptoms may begin on maturing bulbs just before or during harvest.

Control: Avoid using excessive nitrogen fertilizer, which delays maturity. Allow the tops to mature well before harvest. Avoid injury to the bulbs when harvesting. Dry the bulbs before placing them in storage.

Pink Rot.
Pathogen: Pyrenochaeta terrestris fungus.
Symptoms: Roots turn yellow, then turn bright pink and die. This disease can appear in seedlings, or later throughout the season. New roots produced also turn pink and die. The bulbs are reduced in size and vigor. The tops are stunted.

Control: Practice crop rotation where possible. Maintain vigor with proper fertilization and watering. Use of resistant varieties may be helpful.

PEAS

Insecticides for Use on Peas

Bacillus thuringinensis (Dipel, Thuricide) (0 days from application to harvest) A biological control agent for use on caterpillars.

Cygon (0 days from application to harvest) A systemic insecticide, excellent for aphids. Use is limited by protective clothing needed for application.

Diazinon (0 days from application to harvest)

Di-Syston (50 day from application to harvest) A systemic insecticide, excellent for aphids control. Apply at planting; wear protective gloves when applying.

Malathion (3 days from application to harvest)

Methoxychlor (7 days from application to harvest)

Pyrethrin (0 days from application to harvest) An organic insecticide with a very short control period. Generally found in ready-to-use formulations.

Rotenone (1 day from application to harvest) An organic insecticide with a short control period.

Sevin (0 days from application to harvest)

Thiodan (0 days from application to harvest)

Insects of Peas

Aphids—see Aphids.

Cutworms—see Caterpillars - Cutworms.

Pea Weevil. Adult weevils are grayish or grayish-brown and speckled with white, gray and black patches. They are about 1/5-inch long, chunky, with parallel sides. The larvae are white with small brown heads, about 1/16- to 1/4-inch long. The adults spend the winter in protected areas around the garden.

Adults feed on nectar and pollen, causing no direct damage to the pea crop. Eggs are laid on the pea pods. Upon hatching, the larvae bore through the wall of the pods and into the developing peas. The larvae grow and pupate inside the peas, emerging as adults in 6-9 weeks. A small, dark spot or "sting" marks the point of entry on the pea. Infected peas are not desirable for use as food. Most home gardeners, however, do not notice the infestation.

Control: Damage from this pest is common but usually minor. Watch for this pest when the peas average one blossom per plant. Where treatment is needed, spray the foliage during early bloom period. Common insecticides like *Malathion, Methoxychlor, Sevin* or *Rotenone* can be used. Insecticides must be applied to kill the adults before they lay eggs. Once eggs are laid on the pods it is too late to prevent weevil injury. No known natural enemies of importance are present in the United States.

Diseases of Peas

Damping Off.

Pathogen: Pythium fungus.

Symptoms: Seeds rot in ground, failing to come up. Young seedlings suddenly wilt, fall over and die at soil line.

Control: Gardeners will frequently experience this problem in cool wet years. Avoid planting in cool, wet soil. Use treated seeds *(Captan, Thiram* or *Terrachlor).*

Powdery Mildew.

Pathogen: Erisyphe polygoni fungus.

Symptoms: White fungal growth on the surface of leaves and stems looks like the leaves have been dipped in flour. On some varieties the affected area may die. Some pods may develop small necrotic (brown) spots. If infected early, the plants are stunted. This disease is only occasionally seen in the spring, but is very common on fall plantings.

Control: Use of resistant varieties may be helpful. If necessary, apply sulfur at 7-14 day intervals.

Root Rot.

Pathogen: Several fungus organisms could be involved, including *Fusarium* and *Pythium,* which live in the soil.

Symptoms: Plants become yellowish and unthrifty. The underground portion of stems and the roots turn yellow-brown, red or black. Plants often die at flowering time.

Control: Practice crop rotation where possible. Plant in well-drained soils, avoid over-irrigation and drought stress. The use of resistant varieties may be helpful.

PEPPERS

Pollination: Insect pollination is required for pepper production. When applying insecticides, use caution to protect the pollinating insects.

Insecticides for Use on Peppers

Bacillus thuringinensis (Dipel, Thuricide) (0 days from application to harvest) A biological control agent for caterpillars.

Cygon (0 days from application to harvest) To protect bees, do not apply when the crop is in bloom. This is an excellent systemic insecticide for sucking insects. Use is limited by protective clothing needed for application.

Diazinon (5 days from application to harvest) To protect bees, do not apply when crop is in bloom.

Malathion (3 days from application to harvest) When crops are in bloom; apply only in late evening when bees are not active.

Methoxychlor (1 day from application to harvest) When crops are in bloom; apply only from late evening to early morning, when bees are not active.

Pyrethrin (0 days from application to harvest) An organic insecticide with a short control period

Rotenone (1 day from application to harvest) An organic insecticide.

Sevin (0 days from application to harvest) To protect bees, do not apply when the crop is in bloom. Not recommended for use on peppers due to mite build-up following use.

Thiodan (4 days from application to harvest) When the crop is in bloom; apply only from late evening to early morning when the bees are not active.

Insects of Peppers

Aphids—see Aphids.
Cutworms—see Caterpillars - Cutworms.
Flea Beetles—see Potatoes - Flea Beetle.

Diseases of Peppers

Blossom End Rot—see Tomatoes - Blossom End Rot.
Curly Top Virus—see Tomatoes - Curly Top Virus.
Dry Mildew—see Tomatoes - Dry Mildew.
Mosaic Virus. *Pathogen:* Mosaic virus.

Symptoms: Leaves show a mottling of yellow and green; they curl and become distorted. Early season infections result in stunted plants with few fruits. Infected fruits often yellow, shrivel or show an irregular mottled spotting.

Control: Practice rigid weed control in and around the garden (to reduce sources of the virus). Control aphids which spread the virus. Wash your hands after handling infested plants. Do not smoke around plants (they can pick-up the virus from the tobacco smoke). Use of resistant varieties (i.e., "Yolo Wonder," "Pennbell," "Bellboy," "California Wonder 300," and "Keystone Giant") may be helpful.

Phytothphora Root Rot.
Pathogen: Phytothphora capsici fungus.

Symptoms: Dark green water-soaked spots develop at soil level, turning brown as they dry. Plant stems can be girdled and the plant dies. Small dark-green water-soaked leaf spots will enlarge and take on a scaled appearance. Similar spots can develop on the fruit, showing a white fungus growth as the disease progresses. Fruit shrivels but remains attached to the stem.

Control: There is no cure for diseased plants, so remove and destroy all that are infected. Practice crop rotation where possible. The fungus lives in the soil, so do not plow in nor compost diseased plants. The disease is most active in moist, warm weather.

Sunburn on Fruit.
Symptoms: Light tan, leathery spots on fruits, primarily on the south and southwest sides, are caused by sunburn of tender tissues.

Control: None. Cut out the damaged area when using the pepper.

Verticillium Wilt—see Tomatoes - Verticillium Wilt.

POTATOES

Insecticides for Use on Potatoes

Bacillus thuringinensis (0 days from application to harvest) A biological control agent for caterpillars.

Cygon (0 days from application to harvest) A systemic insecticide which is excellent for aphid control. Use is limited by protective clothing needed for application.

Diazinon (35 days from application to harvest)

Di-Syston (75 days from application to harvest) An excellent systemic insecticide to be applied at planting time. Wear protective gloves when applying.

Malathion (0 days from application to harvest)

Pyrethrin (0 days from application to harvest) An organic insecticide with a short control period.

Rotenone (1 day from application to harvest) An organic insecticide.

Sevin (0 days from application to harvest) Not recommended for use on potatoes due to mite build-up following application.

Thiodan (0 days from application to harvest)

Insects of Potatoes

Aphids—see Aphids.
Cabbage Loopers—see Caterpillars.
Colorado Potato Beetle. Adult beetles are 3/8-inch long, rounded, reddish yellow, with 10 black stripes. The plump larvae or grub is brick-red, hump backed, and up to 3/5-inch long. Bright yellow-orange eggs are laid in clusters on the underside of leaves. These pests spend the winter as adults in the soil, emerging in the warming spring days.

Adults and larvae defoliate potatoes. They are especially destructive to small plantings. They may also be a pest on tomatoes, peppers, eggplants, petunias and nicotiana.

Control: Watch for these pests all season, and spray whenever you find them. They can multiply rapidly, causing serious defoliation when left untreated. It is much easier to keep their population down than to stop it once it gets out of hand. Even though you have good control from a spray, don't forget to watch for re-infestation from hatching eggs. (Remember, insecticides do not kill eggs!) Follow-up sprays at 10-14 day intervals are usually needed. Be sure to get complete coverage, including the underside of lower leaves where these pests prefer to hide.

Common garden sprays are helpful. *Sevin* is good, but not recommended due to spider mite build-up following its use. You'll have good results with *Cygon,* fair results with *Diazinon, Malathion, Rotenone* and *Thiodan.* If you have chronic problems with these pests you may want to try *Di-Syston.* It is good, but can only be applied at planting. Organically, hand picking is listed for control, but with this approach it may be difficult to keep up.

Colorado Potato Beetle: adult (left) and larvae (right) (Photo: U.S.D.A. Extension Service)

Cutworms—see Caterpillars - Cutworms.

Flea Beetles. Adults of the various species are similar in appearance; being small (1/16-inch long), hard-shelled, shiny, dark-colored beetles that jump (hence the common name) when disturbed. These adults spend the winter in sheltered areas under surface debris. Initial feeding in the spring occurs on various weeds, but the beetles move to the garden as soon as host plants appear. Eggs are deposited in the soil and hatch within 10 days. The slender, whitish, cylindrical larvae feed in or on roots, tubers, and underground stems for 3-4 weeks. Full-grown larvae are up to 1/3-inch long, with brown heads. Pupation occurs in the soil, and new adults emerge in 1-2 weeks. There are two generations produced each year.

Larvae feeding on root systems causes stunting and can reduce production, but significant larval damage is generally noticed only on potatoes. Larvae feed on the surface of the tuber and may penetrate up to 1/2-inch into it. Surface damage shows as narrow, irregular, winding trails. Internal damage appears as narrow, brown tunnels referred to as "slivers." These tunnels often serve as entry points for various rot organisms.

Adult feeding on most plants appears as small, round pinholes eaten out of the leaves. Beetle feeding on corn leaves appears as thin, irregular, white stripes where the upper surface of the leaf has been removed. Under severe infestation, the leaves may be completely consumed. Small plants may be killed, and larger plants will be stunted. Flea beetles also serve as vectors of various plant diseases.

One or more species of flea beetles may attack a variety of garden plants including potatoes, eggplants, tomatoes, beans, beets, cabbage, carrots, celery, corn, cucumber, lettuce, melons, pumpkins, radishes, raspberries, rhubarb, spinach, sunflowers, sweet potatoes, and watermelon. Potatoes are often the most severely damaged.

Control: Where needed, early season application of foliar insecticides should be aimed to control adults before the eggs can be deposited. *Diazinon, Di-Syston, Malathion, Methoxychlor, Pyrethrin, Rotenone, Sevin* and *Thiodan* can be used. *Diazinon* granules incorporated into the soil at planting time offer some protection against larval feeding.

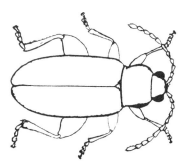

Flea Beetle. (Picture: U.S.D.A. Extension Service)

Leafhoppers—see Leafhoppers.

Spider Mites—see Spider Mites.

White Grubs. Grubs or larvae are white or light yellow, with brown heads, curved bodies and three pairs of legs. They are 1/2-inch to 1 1/2-inches long when full grown. White grubs which live in soil generally take three years to mature. The adults are known as June Bugs or May Beetles. They are large, reddish-brown or black beetles about an inch long. They emerge in late spring or early summer, and feed on the foliage of trees and shrubs. The adults fly at night, being attracted to lights, and often invade the home. Eggs are laid in the soil.

The grubs feed on roots and underground parts of potato and many other plants. Adults prefer to feed on the foliage of hardwood trees.

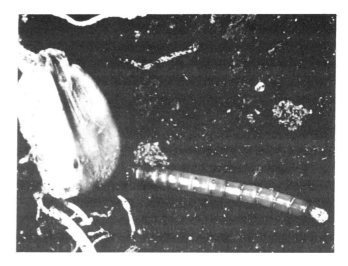

White Grub larvae (left) and Wireworm larvae (right) (Photo: U.S.D.A. Extension Service)

Control: Where this is a problem, broadcast and cultivate *Diazinon* granules into the soil before planting.

Wireworms—*Elateridae* family of beetles.

Wireworms are the larvae of click beetles. They are hard-shelled, reddish-brown, smooth, and wire-like in appearance; or they can be soft-bodied, white, with yellowish-brown heads and tails. They usually range from 3/8- to 1-inch in length.

The adult Click Beetle is elongated, tapering to the end and hard-shelled. Their name comes from their ability to flip into the air in an effort to right themselves when placed on their backs. Depending on the species, they are 1/4- to 1 1/4-inches long, and tan to black in color.

They take 2-5 years in the larvae stage before emerging as adults, thus their population slowly builds. These pests live in the soil, moving up and down in depth depending on temperature and moisture.

Adults do little feeding. The larvae feed on all underground portions of a wide variety of plants. Feeding on seeds prevents germination. Feeding on young plants usually kills them. More established plants are stunted by the wireworms' feeding. Their damage provides a source of entry for disease organisms. Potatoes are the crop most seriously damaged where the wireworms produce round holes, up to 1/8-inch in diameter, straight into the tubers.

Control: Wireworms are most common in uncultivated soils or in grain fields. In garden settings, the damage is generally most severe when the garden is first put under cultivation.

Where damage is at critical levels, the population can be reduced by cultivating *Diazinon* granules into the soil prior to planting.

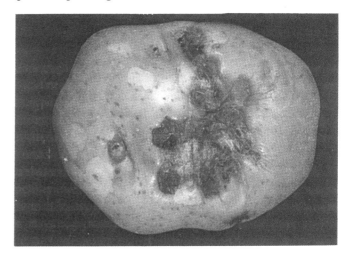

Black Leg disease of potato vines (left) and Scab on Tubers (right). (Photos: U.S.D.A. Extension Service)

Diseases of Potatoes

Black Leg.

Pathogen: Erwinia atroseptica bacteria.

Symptoms: Leaves curl upwards and yellow. As the disease progresses, dark, inky black and sometimes slimy

lesions extend up the stems for some distance above the ground. These lesions can also extend downward into the developing tubers. In warm, moist weather, the disease progresses rapidly and the entire plant wilts and dies.

When tubers are affected, the rot begins at the stem end. Tuber lesions are small and dark; often only a small, circular black opening is visible on the surface. In the interior of the potato, a progressive decaying area develops in an irregular, black, soft or slimy hollow. Affected tubers decay rapidly in wet soils.

Control: The bacteria is carried on apparently healthy seed pieces, lives in infected soils, and can be transmitted by tuber-feeding insects. Thus, use only healthy certified seed potatoes. Cut tubers into 2-3 oz. pieces, allowing them to suberize before planting. Do not plant in cool, wet soils; avoid over-watering and over-fertilization. Practice crop rotation where practical; never plow in or compost diseased plants.

Common Scab.

Pathogen: Streptomyces scabies bacteria.

Symptoms: Scab is a very common disease of potatoes in the alkali soils of the West. It has no influence on yield, but the severely blemished tubers lack appeal. Corky lesions develop on the tuber surface. They may be small, or large and pitted. Infected tubers are often described as looking dirty, but the lesions will not wash off.

Soils with a high calcium level (as found in the Inter-mountain West's Great Basin) and soils rich in non-decomposed organic matter (like fresh manure) favor the disease. Dry soils, particularly during the early growing season, will also favor common scab development.

In addition to potatoes, the scab pathogen may infect beets, radishes, turnips, rutabagas and carrots.

Control: This disease has no direct control; the University of Idaho Extension Service suggests the following cultural practices to reduce its severity. The bacteria lives in the soil, so practice crop rotation to the extent possible. Use only certified seed potatoes when planting to avoid picking up the bacteria on infected seed pieces. Avoid adding fresh organic matter into the potato patch. On high lime (calcium) soils (common to the Great Basin), scab can be significantly suppressed by maintaining high soil phosphate. High soil moisture will also help suppress common scab. The most critical time for careful irrigation is from 2 to 7 weeks after emergence. Russet varieties generally are less affected than smooth-skinned varieties.

Early Blight.

Pathogen: Alternaria solani fungus.

Symptoms: Early Blight is a common foliar disease of potatoes. It produces dark-brown to black-colored spots on leaves and stems. The spots first appear as small specks and gradually increase in size, sometimes exceeding one-half inch in diameter. They are generally irregular in shape. Some may be angular where they border larger veins. Ordinarily a series of concentric target-like rings form within the lesion. A yellowish border may form around the dark spots. Older leaves, those nearest the ground, become infected first. Tuber spots occur less often. They are small, sunken, brown or black spots with an underlying brown corky dry rot.

Control: Since Early Blight is the most common disease of potatoes in the West, routinely keep your eye open for it, checking lower leaves for spots weekly. It often starts in late June, with serious problems developing in late July. Early Blight spotting on the stems in August is an indication that the disease is getting out of control.

Early Blight can be controlled by a few applications of fungicides like *Daconil* or *Maneb*. Generally two to three applications at 10-14 day intervals will suffice. Complete coverage, including lower leaves, is essential for control.

Heavy thick foliage which keeps the leaves moist, water stress, a lack of nitrogen fertilizer, or Verticillium wilt will enhance the blight development. Light, mid-summer applications of a nitrogen fertilizer, like ammonium sulfate, will help maintain plant vigor. Sprinkler irrigation can enhance its spread. Remove and destroy infected vines at harvest.

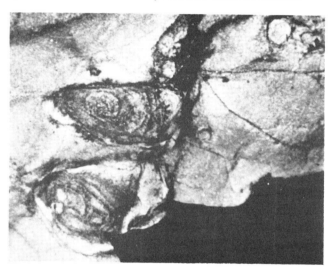

Target-like rings of Early Blight on a potato and tomato. (Photo: U.S.D.A. Extension Service)

Potato Leaf Roll Virus.

Pathogen: Potato Leaf Roll Virus.

Symptoms: As the name implies, leafrolling is the main symptom in plants grown from infected seed tubers. In most varieties, the first symptoms become noticeable about a month after the plants emerge. The leaflets of the lower leaves roll up at the edges and become somewhat papery, brittle, and leathery to the touch. Affected leaves rattle if brushed with the hand. As the plant grows, the rolling appears on the higher leaves and eventually affects the whole plant. The rolled leaves are lighter in color than healthy ones. In some varieties, a reddish or purple discoloration occurs on the leaf undersides. Plants often become dwarfed. Yields can be reduced by as much as one-half.

Leafroll virus is transmitted from plant to plant by the green peach aphid. Plants which become infected during the season often remain symptomless. However, the tubers will develop net necrosis (brown strands of tissue in a net pattern) through the tuber. This can develop before or after harvest. Cooks commonly see this discoloration when peeling potatoes.

Control: There is no cure for diseased plants. The following cultural practices will help keep Leafroll Virus under control. 1) Control aphids which transmit the virus. 2) Control mustards and other weeds around the garden which harbor the virus. 3) Remove plants showing symptoms. 4) Plant certified seed only. 5) Destroy volunteer potatoes.

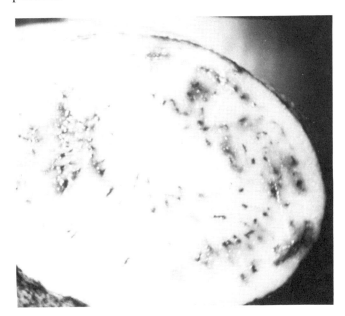

Rolled and yellow leaves of a potato plant infected with Leafroll Virus (left). Net necrosis symptom of Leafroll virus on tuber (right). (Photos: U.S.D.A. Extension Service)

Bacterial Soft Rot.

Pathogen: Erwinia carotovora bacteria.

Symptoms: Bacterial soft rot is common to potatoes, carrots and other vegetables. Infections from the seed piece can cause the tuber to rot in the ground before emerging. Leaves on infected plants curl upward, gradually yellow and die. Mushy, light brown to colorless lesions form at the base of the stems. Gardeners are more familiar with symptoms on the tubers. Affected tissues of tubers are typically white to cream colored, soft and somewhat watery—especially if the decay developed under moist conditions. A clear, amber liquid often exudes from the decayed part. The slimy decay may progress into either a wet-rot stage or dry up into a chalky white lesion. Infected tubers break down partially or completely and a slimy, foul-smelling rot may develop.

Control: Use only healthy certified seed potatoes. Cut the tubers into 2-3 oz. pieces, allowing them to be suberized before planting. Do not plant in cool, wet soils and avoid over-watering. Practice crop rotation where practical.

The key to controlling bacterial soft rot in storage is careful handling at harvest to prevent wounds, cuts, cracks or bruises. Harvest potatoes in dry weather to promote rapid drying and healing of wounds and thus eliminate entry sites for the soft-rot bacterium. Avoid sun scald of the tubers. If potatoes require washing, quickly squirt off the dirt and allow them to dry; avoid soaking the tubers. Store tubers below 45 degrees, with good ventilation.

Verticillium Wilt or Early Die.

Pathogen: Verticillium albo-atrum fungus.

Symptoms: This common disease shows up in many gardens each year. The vascular tissues (the tissues in which water moves just under the surface) turn dark. Plants turn yellow and dry up early. The yellowing may be on one side only or on the entire plant. Yields are reduced.

Control: High-nitrogen fertilizer will help suppress the symptoms. Add summer nitrogen sidedressings to maintain good green color (see fertilizers). The fungus lives in the soil, so do not plow in or compost diseased plants. Practice crop rotation where possible.

RADISHES AND TURNIPS

Insecticides for Use on Radishes and Turnips

Bacillus thuringinensis (0 days from application to harvest) An excellent biological control agent for caterpillars.

Chlorban (Dursban granules) (apply at planting time) Excellent for root maggot control.

Diazinon (10 days from application to harvest)

Malathion (7 days from application to harvest)

Methoxychlor (7 days from application to harvest, 14 days on turnip tops)

Pyrethrin (0 days from application to harvest) An organic insecticide with a short control period.

Sevin (3 days from application to harvest, 14 days on turnip tops)

Insects of Radishes and Turnips

Aphids—see Aphids.

Cutworms—see Caterpillars - Cutworms.

Flea Beetles—see Potatoes - Flea Beetles.

Cabbage Root Maggot.

This is the common, white, root feeding maggot of radishes and turnips. It also feeds on cabbage, broccoli, Brussel sprouts, beets, celery and other vegetables.

Adult flies emerge from the soil in May, about the time sweet cherries bloom. They are 1/4-inch long, gray, with black stripes on the thorax (region below the head). Eggs are laid on the base of host plants and in the surrounding soil. The leg-less larvae or maggot feeds on the host plant roots for about three weeks, riddling the roots with brown tunnels. They then pupate in the soil, and the cycle continues around again. Two or three generations can occur each year. Winter is spent as pupa in the upper soil.

Control: Cool, moist weather favors infestations. Early transplanted cabbage and broccoli, late spring radishes, and early turnips are generally hit hardest. Very early radishes and late cabbage and broccoli may escape. Covering the seed beds with cheesecloth may provide some protection from egg-laying flies.

Diazinon granules applied at planting has been an old standard for maggot control, giving fair to poor results. Spraying the plant generally gives little help.

Maggot-free crops are easy to grow now with the recent registration of *Chlorban (dursban)* granules. Washington State University researchers report good results when it is applied with the seed at planting. On radishes, the *Chlorban* 0.5% granular label calls for approximately 4 tablespoons per 10-feet of row, applied with the seed into the furrow.

On turnips, cabbage and broccoli, the 0.5% *Chlorban* label calls for approximately 1/2 cup per 10 feet of row. Place it over the seed in a 2-4-inch wide band, at planting time followed by a watering. It may not give satisfactory long-term control on turnips.

Slugs—see Slugs and Snails.

SPINACH

Insecticides for Use on Spinach

Bacillus thuringiensis (B.t., Dipel, Thuricide) (0 days from application to harvest) A biological control insecticide for use on caterpillars.

Cygon (14 days from application to harvest) A systemic insecticide, excellent for aphids. Use is limited by protective clothing needed for application.

Diazinon (10 days from application to harvest)

Malathion (7 days from application to harvest)

Sevin (14 days from application to harvest)

Insects of Spinach

Aphids—see Aphids.

Cutworms—see Caterpillars - Cutworms.

Flea Beetles—see Potatoes - Flea Beetles.

Spinach Leaf Miners, *Pegomya hyoscyami.*

Small whitish maggots feed between the leaf surfaces making winding tunnels or mines. Mines are gradually enlarged and may emerge to form large light-colored blotched areas with dark excrement inside. Feeding lasts for 1-3 weeks, and more than one maggot may feed in a

Spinach Leaf Miner Damage in beets. (Photo: David Whiting)

single leaf. Maggots may also move from leaf to leaf as they feed. Pupation (the cocoon stage) may occur in the leaf or in the soil.

Adults emerge in 2-4 weeks as slender, gray flies 1/4-inch long. Elongated white eggs, laid on the underside of host leaves, hatch in 3-4 days. The cycle continues again, with three or more generations per season. Winter is spent as cocoons in the soil.

This pest is common on spinach, chard, beets, and related weeds. Heavy feeding renders the leaves unfit for use and decreases beet size.

Control: A light population may be controlled with hand removal of eggs and infested leaves. This should be done every couple of days to keep on top of the problem.

Cheesecloth tents over the spinach, chard and beet crops can screen out the fly, if carefully placed. Control host weeds, likes lambs-quarter, to reduce local populations. Very early and fall plantings often have less pressure from this pest.

Repeated spraying with insecticides like *Diazinon* or *Malathion* may give some relief under heavy attack. The sprays will be helpful in killing the adult flies as they rest on the leaves; however, they will not be effective in controlling eggs nor the maggots inside the leaf! You will find, however, that spraying every 10 to 14 days interferes with your harvest.

Cabbage Loopers—see Caterpillars.

TOMATOES

Pollination: Tomatoes are pollinated by plant movement (wind) and insects. When applying insecticides, use caution to protect the pollinating insects.

Insecticides for Use on Tomatoes

Bacillus thuringinensis (Dipel, Thuricide) (0 days from application to harvest) A biological insecticide for use on caterpillars.

Cygon (7 days from application to harvest) To protect bees, do not apply when the crop is in bloom. Use is limited by protective clothing needed for applications.

Diazinon (1 day from application to harvest) To protect bees, do not apply when the crop is in bloom.

Di-Syston (30 days from application to harvest) Wear protective gloves when applying. An excellent systemic insecticide.

Malathion (1 day from application to harvest) When crop is in bloom, apply only in late evening when bees are not active.

Pyrethrin (0 days from application to harvest) An organic insecticide with a very short control period.

Rotenone (1 day from application to harvest) An organic insecticide.

Sevin (0 days from application to harvest) To protect bees, do not apply when the crop is in bloom. Not recommended due to mite build-up following use.

Thiodan (1 day from application to harvest) When crop is in bloom, apply only from late evening to early morning when bees are not active.

Insects of Tomatoes

Aphids—see Aphids.
Beet Leafhopper—see Leafhoppers.
Cutworms—see Caterpillars - Cutworms.
Drosophila Fruit Fly or **Vinegar Gnats.**
Adults are tiny yellowish flies or gnats, usually not more

than 3- or 4-mm in length. They are common around decaying or fermenting produce, in which their eggs are laid and maggots develop.

This pest is common around fruit, garbage cans, tomato patches, etc. Eggs and maggots contaminate food products.

Control: Flies will invade crushed, broken or rotting fruits. Keep all ripe fruit picked up or harvested. Control other insects which damage fruit. When insecticides are necessary, spray the fruit and soil with *Malathion* or *Thiodan*.

Flea Beetles—see Potatoes - Flea Beetles.
Loopers and other Caterpillars—see Caterpillars.
Spider Mites—see Spider Mites.
Whitefly, *Aleyrodidae* family.

Whitefly adults have two pairs of rounded wings covered with a pure white waxy powder. They are about 1/8-inch long and have the appearance of a miniature moth. They actually are not flies nor moths, but are of the order Homoptera, as are aphids and scale. They congregate on the underside of leaves, flying out in clouds when the plant is disturbed.

The young or nymphs change in appearance with each molting (skin shed). They are active, oval, whitish and semi-transparent. The white eggs are 1/100-inch long.

Whiteflies feed on plant sap, causing leaves and fruit to become sticky with their honeydew. Whiteflies are generally a sub-tropical pest, so relatively few of them are seen in the Intermountain West. They feed on tomatoes, cucumbers, coleus, begonias and occasionally on other garden plants. Whiteflies are more common in greenhouse growing where they are protected from the cold.

Control: This pest is very difficult to control. Sprays of *Resmethrin* are the insecticide of choice. *Cygon, Thiodan, Malathion,* and *Pyrethrin* are fair. Complete coverage, including the underside of leaves, is essential for control.

Whitefly (Photo U.S.D.A. Extension Service)

Diseases of Tomatoes

Bacterial Speck.

Pathogen: Pseudomonas syringae tomato bacteria.

Symptoms: Numerous black specks about 1/16-inch long appear on leaves, stems and fruit; a pale zone borders the spots. On fruit the specks are slightly raised but do not extend into the flesh. This disease is occasionally observed under wet conditions. Similar symptoms appear with Early Blight.

Control: The disease occurs when temperatures are in the 60-70 degree range and rains are common. Splashing rain and the movement of equipment and people through the tomato paths assist in the entrance and spread of the bacteria into the plants. Clean up the weeds around the garden which harbor the bacteria. Bactericides are not generally warranted.

Blossom End Rot.

Pathogen: caused by a water imbalance.

Symptoms: Blossom-end rot is a sunken, dark, leathery spot on the bottom or "blossom end" of the tomato fruit. It affects green as well as ripe fruits, being more common on the ripe. Peppers are also susceptible.

Blossom-end rot is a very common physiological disorder which results from an imbalance in water and calcium. It is not insect nor disease related, and is not related to the position of the fruit to the ground. Affected fruit can be used by cutting away the damaged portion.

Control: Blossom-end rot is associated with a temporary shortage of calcium in the fruit. It is caused or aggravated by low or by excessively high soil moisture. In the Intermountain West, where soils are naturally high in lime (calcium), the control is centered around water management.

Moisture problems which interfere with the balance of calcium salts in the plant are common on both sandy and clay soils. Sandy soils, with their low ability to store water, can easily dry too much between waterings. Heavy clay soils and soils with poor drainage can be easily over-irrigated.

Tomatoes on rich, deep soils should receive a thorough watering, wetting the soil 24" deep. In typical summer weather, this would be about once a week on loam and clay soils, about twice a week on sandy loam soils, and every 2-3 days on sand. The watering pattern should be adjusted to weather conditions and for shallow soils. Often a slight adjustment in the irrigation pattern will correct the disorder; water a little less or a little more often.

Using a mulch (plastic or organic) will help stabilize the moisture supply. Soil cultivations which cut feeder roots may attribute to Blossom-end Rot. Large fluctuations in the daily summer temperature can stimulate it. Often the disorder corrects itself with a change in the summer's weather pattern.

Excessive fertilizer applications which stimulate vegetative growth may aggravate it. This is particularly true on acid soils and where heavy applications of ammonium-based nitrogens are applied just as fruiting begins. The heavy use of manure, especially from poultry, may favor this condition. Tomato varieties differ in susceptibility; pear-shaped varieties are more susceptible.

In acid soil areas, low soil calcium is routinely corrected with the addition of LIME (calcium) added to raise the pH.

Spraying fruit and foliage with a calcium chloride gives variable results in controlling blossom-end rot. Use calcium chloride (77% product) at a rate of 1 tablespoon per gallon of water on 100 feet of row. Sprays are needed before and during stress periods of heat and drought. Make 1 or 2 applications per week. But keep in mind that these sprays can cause foliage injury from the salts.

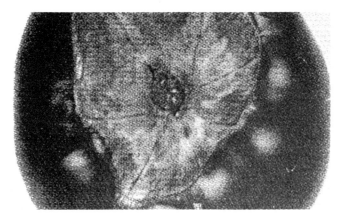

Blossom-end Rot on tomato (Photo: U.S.D.A. Extension Service).

Buckeye Rot.
Pathogen: Phytothphora parasitica fungus.
Symptoms: The most characteristic symptom is a large discolored spot on the lower fruit. The spot usually has pale brown concentric rings in a target pattern. The skin is not rotted, but a semi-watery decay may extend to the fruit's center.
Control: Plant in well drained soils. Use special care in irrigation to achieve even soil moisture; avoid wet soil conditions. Practice crop rotation where practical.

Curly Top Virus.
Pathogen: Curly Top Virus.
Symptoms: Upward curling and twisting of leaflets, stiff and leathery foliage that is uniformly yellowish. Veins become dominant and purplish. Plants are stunted. Fruits ripen prematurely before they reach normal size. This common disease attacks plants at random; just a plant here and there. The virus is spread by the Beet Leafhopper.
Control: There is no cure for diseased plants. Remove the infected plants to reduce the spread. Control weeds to help reduce leafhopper populations (see Leafhoppers). Since tomatoes are not the preferred host of the Beet Leafhopper, spraying tomatoes to control the hopper is not very helpful.

Dry Mildew of Tomato.
Pathogen: Leveillula taurica fungus.
Symptoms: It first shows up in July as distinct *bright* yellow spots on the leaves. These spots are 1/8- to 1/4-inch in diameter. The spots eventually enlarge, grow together and turn brown. As the pathogen continues to grow, it causes the entire leaf to wither and die *but remain attached to the stem.* There are no symptoms on the stems or fruits. In fact, fruits from diseased plants look and taste normal. However, the loss of leaves exposes the fruits to sunburn. In severely infected plants, only a tuft of terminal leaves remain alive. Fruit on infected plants fails to grow to normal size. Plants may partially recover and resume growth in the fall as temperatures cool off and rains become more frequent. The disease is more prevalent in dry, hot summers with occasional rain storms.

Dry mildew of tomato can be easily confused with Early Blight. With Early Blight, leaves are a lighter yellow, with distinct halo or target markings in the dominate brown spots; the leaves fall off.
Control: Use only locally grown transplants. The disease is brought into the Utah area each year on bare-root plants. Sulfur sprays or dusts are effective if complete coverage starts early (when sprouts are less than 1/4-inch) and where sprays are repeated every 7 to 14 days. However, sulfur can burn the plants if applied when temperatures are high—above 95 degrees. If tomatoes are to be canned in metal containers, do not apply sulfur within 40 days of harvest.

Curly Top Virus on Tomato (left). Dry Mildew on tomato (right).

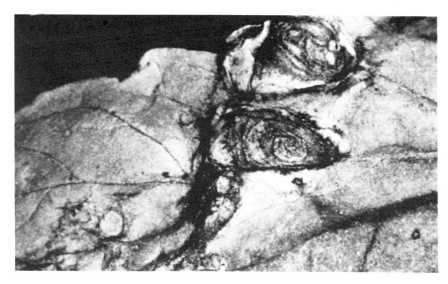

Early Blight leaf spots on Tomato; note the target-like rings on the spots.
(Photo: U.S.D.A. Extension Service)

Early Blight.

Pathogen: Alternaria solani fungus.

Symptoms: Leaf symptoms begin as pinpoint-size brown-to-black spots, usually on the older leaves. The spots may have yellow borders. Concentric target-like rings of light and dark brown can be seen as the spots enlarge. Similar spots develop on the stem and may girdle the plant. Spots on the fruit are similar, generally developing at the stem end.

Early Blight is a common disease of tomatoes and potatoes and can also attack peppers and eggplants. It is aggravated by warm wet weather and where heavy foliage delays the drying of the leaves.

Control: Since the fungus lives in plant debris, do not plow in diseased plants. Practice crop rotation where possible. Destroy volunteer potatoes and tomatoes which can harbor the fungus.

Maintain good plant vigor with adequate fertilizer. Healthy vigorous plants are more resistant. Remember that over-fertilizing tomatoes will lead to excessive vine growth at the expense of fruiting. But tomatoes do like very light fertilizer applications (see fertilizers).

Avoid crowding plants. They need good air circulation to dry the leaves quickly. General spacing is 2 feet or more on trellised vines and 3-4 feet for non-trellised plants. Wet weather and sprinkler irrigation can facilitate the disease spread.

This disease is very common, so keep a close eye on your tomatoes and spray immediately if spotting begins. Fungicides like *Daconil, Maneb* and *Zineb* are effective. Complete coverage, including the lower leaves, is essential for control. Repeat at 14-day intervals, as needed. Under sprinkler irrigation conditions, frequent rains or rapid spread, 7-day intervals would be necessary. If this disease gets out of hand, it is very hard to stop.

Tobacco Mosaic Virus.

Pathogen: Tobacco Mosaic Virus.

Symptoms: Leaves show a mottling of yellow, light green and dark green; they may curl and look deformed. Edges of the leaves often turn down and stiffen. The fruit is small, deformed and sparse.

Tobacco Mosaic Virus attacks tomatoes, peppers, eggplants, petunias and nearly any solanaceous plant. The virus is mechanically transmitted, that is spread by insects, tools, people, etc. moving through the plants. A common source of the virus is tobacco smoke. The virus can rub off the clothing and hands of smokers as they work in the garden.

Control: Do not smoke around the garden. Remove infected plants and wash your hands after handling any symptomatic plants. Control all weeds in the tomato/potato family, which harbors the virus.

2,4-D Injury.

Pathogen: Injury from the drift of 2,4-D herbicide

Symptoms: 2,4-D herbicide is the lawn weed spray used for broadleaf weed control, like the control of dandelions. Leaves emerging at the time of the herbicide's drift are curled and twisted, with the veins showing a distinctive parallel pattern rather than the normal fan pattern. Older leaves may be yellowed or browned. Fruit may be deformed. The extent of damage depends on the p.p.m. of 2,4-D picked up by plants. 2,4-D drift is common and can move for several yards on a warm day with even a light wind. Leaching of 2,4-D with soil moisture can also be a problem.

Control: This is the most common problem home gardeners have with tomatoes. Tomatoes and grapes are very sensitive. Avoid spraying lawn areas adjacent to gardens. Avoid using 2,4-D in the summer time, when temperatures are above 90 degrees. Avoid spraying on windy days, since even the slightest wind will cause the

2,4-D to drift. Mildly affected plants may out-grow the damage.

Furasrium Wilt and Verticillium Wilt.

Pathogen: Verticillium albo-artum or *Fusarium oxysporum* fungus.

Symptoms: Symptoms and control of both diseases are similar. Laboratory identification of the fungus is necesary to distinguish between the two.

Leaf symptoms begin as a general drooping, wilting and yellowing of the lower leaves. As the disease progresses up the stem, successive leaves yellow, wilt and die. The plant may become stunted, permanently wilt and die; the brown leaves remain attached to the stem. Symptoms may show on the entire plant or only on portions. The leaf symptoms can easily be confused with early blight.

The best diagnostic symptom is to look for "vascular discoloration" (browning of the tissue along the stem just under the skin). To do this, take the lower stem segment of the wilted plant, cut it lengthwise, or peel back the heavy bark-like skin. Diseased plants will show a brown discoloration in the woody tissue under the skin.

The diseases are erratic, showing to varying degrees from season to season. The fungus live in the soil.

Control: There is no cure for the diseased plants. Since the disease lives in the soil, do not plow in nor compost diseased plants, and practice crop rotation where possible. Many common tomato varieties have resistance to Verticillium and Fusarium. This in indicated in their name or description by using the letters "V" and "F." For example, Jet Star VF tomatoes indicate resistance to both Verticillium and Fusarium. Resistance should not be interpreted as immunity, since there are several strains of each disease.

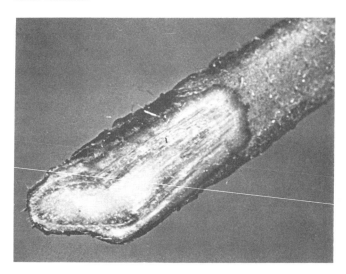

Fusarium Wilt on tomato; vine dieback (left). Cross section of a stem showing necrosis in vascular tissue (right). (Photo: U.S.D.A. Extension Service)

VINE CROPS
Cucumbers, Cantaloupes, Melons, Squash, Pumpkins and Watermelons

Pollination: The vine crop family requires insect pollination. When applying insecticides, use caution to protect the pollinating insects.

Insecticides for Use on Vine Crops

Bacillus thuringiensis (Dipel, Thuricide) (0 days from application to harvest) A biological insecticide for control of caterpillars.

Diazinon (7 days on cucumbers and summer squash; 3 days on melons and winter squash) To protect bees, do not apply when the crop is in bloom.

Malathion (1 day from application to harvest) When crop is in bloom, apply only in late evening when bees are not active.

Methoxychlor (1 day from application to harvest) When crop is in bloom, apply only from late evening to early morning, when the bees are not active.

Rotenone (1 day from application to harvest) An organic insecticide, not highly toxic to bees.

Sevin (0 days from application to harvest) To protect bees, do not apply when the crop is in bloom. Not recommended on vine crops due to mite build-up follcwing use.

Thiodan (0 days from application to harvest) When the crop is in bloom, apply only from late evening to early morning when bees are not active.

NOTE: *do not* apply *diazinon* on pumpkins.

Insects of Vine crops

Aphids—see Aphids.

Cabbage Loopers and other caterpillars—see Caterpillars.

Cucumber Beetles. There are two species of cucumber beetles which commonly attack vine crops in the West, the Western Spotted Cucumber Beetle and the Western Striped Cucumber Beetle. Adults of both species are about 1/4-inch long, with black heads, yellow thorax (the neck-like region behind the head) and yellow wing covers. The spotted species are greenish-yellow, with 12 black spots on their back. The striped beetles are pale orange-yellow, with three longitudinal black stripes on their back. Both species spend the winter as adults and deposit eggs in the

Striped Cucumber Beetles. (Photo: U.S.D.A. Extention Service)

Cutworms—see Caterpillars - Cutworms

Leafhoppers—see Leafhoppers

Spider Mites—see Spider Mites

Squash Bugs. The adults are dark brown to gray, elongated-oval shaped with flat backs, about 5/8-inch long. They become active in late spring, moving into the garden about the time the vine crops begin to put out runners. The eggs are elliptical, 1/16-inch long, yellowish brown turning red, and are primarily laid on the underside of leaves in the "V" formed where the veins merge. The nymphs or young are green with crimson legs, head, and antennae. Older nymphs are more gray, with dark legs and antennae. Both nymphs and adults are capable of producing the "stink bug" odor when disturbed. The pests spend the winter as adults, hiding in protected areas.

Adults and nymphs feed in colonies, generally near the crown of the plant; they suck sap from the leaves and stems. Heavy feeding causes plants to suddenly wilt and die, runner by runner. Winter squash and pumpkins are their preferred diet, but they will attack all vine crops.

Control: Good yard sanitation will often give adequate control. Cleanup the yard early in the fall, before the adults

soil. Eggs hatch in 7-10 days into slender, light-colored, worm-like larvae, growing up to about 1/3-inch.

The larvae bore into roots and stems below the soil line. These pests usually attack young plants, causing the plants to wilt and sometimes to die. Adults feed on the leaves, flowers and stems, causing serious defoliation when the populations are heavy.

Control: Watch for beetles when the plants first appear above the ground. Treat when the insects first appear with common insecticides like *Thiodan, Rotenone, Malathion,* or *Diazinon.* Repeat at 7-10 day intervals as needed. Insecticide applications should be made early enough to prevent significant egg laying.

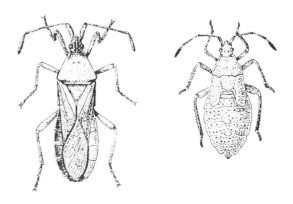

Squash Bug Adult and Nymph. (Picture: U.S.D.A. Extention Service)

find winter homes, by removing surface debris and plant residues.

In the early summer, check in the evening for squash bugs, nymphs and eggs. If only a few plants are involved, light populations can be reduced by hand picking of bugs and eggs. Bugs may be found hiding under boards and other debris.

Squash bugs are difficult to control with insecticides. *Thiodan* and/or *Rotenone* would be first choices. Direct the spray under the leaves and at the crown of the plants. Sprays are more effective if applied when the pests are young.

Thrips—see Thrips.

Diseases of Vine Crops

Blossom Drop. Members of the cucurbit family (squash, cucumbers and melons) have both male and female flowers on the same plant. The female blossom has a baby squash, melon or cucumber behind the flower. If the blossom is not fertilized, the fruit will not develop. The larger male blossom has no fruit, just a long stem.

On most squash, melons and cucumbers, the male

flower dominates, or in other words the vines produce more male flowers than female flowers, and the male flowers generally appear first. *Thus gardeners should understand that first flowers and the majority of flowers, being male, will not set fruit.*

Pollination, meaning the movement of pollen from a male flower to a female flower, results in the growth of fruit. This is usually performed by insects carrying pollen from one flower to another. When insect activity is insufficient, pollination can be achieved by hand. Rub pollen from the center of the male flower onto the center of the female flower. It is simple to do, just pick a male blossom, remove its petals and visit the females.

Some cucumbers produce a majority of female flowers. These are referred to as *"gynoecious"* cucumbers. They have the advantage that they can set fruit from the first blooms.

Gardeners should be extra careful not to use insecticides which will interfere with the activity of bees and other pollinating insects. For example, the use of *Diazinon* or *Sevin* could eliminate bee activity on the plant (see insecticides for vine crops). When applying insecticides, do not directly spray blossoms.

Vine crops will also abort fruit when excessive fruit sets. Any form of stress, such as drought, over-watering, fertilizer excess or deficiency, heat, insects, powdery mildew, etc. will also decrease fruit set.

Large fruits with maturing seeds will slow or cut production. Harvest cucumber and summer squash fruits at a young stage before major seed development occurs.

Damping Off.

Pathogen: Pythium fungus.

Symptoms: Seeds fail to come up, having decayed in the soil. Young plants collapse at the soil line and die. This is a common problem in cool wet springs.

Control: Allow the soil to warm and dry before planting. Use treated seed *(Captan, Thiram* or *Terrachlor).*

Fusarium Wilt.

Pathogen: Fusarium oxysporum fungus.

Symptoms: Plants yellow and wilt; they may partially recover during the night, but wilting progresses until the plant finally withers and dies. A pinkish-white fungal growth may occur on diseased stems near the ground. Vascular discoloration (browning of the internal stem tissues) may occur near the crown. (For more details, see Tomatoes - Fusarium Wilt.)

Control: There is no cure for diseased plants. Since the disease lives in the soil, do not plow in or compost diseased plants. Use of resistant varieties may be helpful. Where soil is infested with *Fusarium* fungus, soil fumigation is the only direct control.

Mosaic Virus.

Pathogen: Mosaic Virus.

Symptoms: Leaves become wrinkled, mottled with yellow and green blotches and cupped downward. Early infection results in dwarfed plants. Fruits have raised, pale, whitish-green, warty lumps.

Control: Remove all infected vines. Control aphids which spread the virus. The use of resistant varieties may be helpful. Control perennial weeds like milkweeds, ground cherry, catnip, etc. which harbor the virus.

Powdery Mildew.

Pathogen: Erysiphe cichoracearum fungus.

Symptoms: White powdery or fuzzy spots appear on leaves and stems, which may grow together covering the entire surface. The symptoms usually occur in scattered spots throughout the planting. This disease is very common, particularly from mid-August into the fall.

Control: Crop rotation is helpful. The use of resistant varieties may be helpful. Powdery Mildew can explode in late August-September as the nights cool off and the night humidity rises. Spray with *Benomyl* when symptoms first appear, repeating at 10-day intervals.

Phytophthora Fruit Rot of Cantaloupe & Watermelon.

Pathogen: Phytophrhora spp. fungus.

Symptoms: Spots develop on the fruit. The skin is not decayed, but internal discoloration may extend into the center of the fruit.

Control: Plant in well-drained soil. Allow the soil to dry between irrigations. Keep the fruit out of irrigation ditches. Spraying is generally not necessary.

Sclerotinia Rot of Squash.

Pathogen: Sclerotinia sclerotiorum fungus.

Symptoms: This disease occurs primarily as a stem blight and fruit rot. A white cottony mold develops on the fruit and stems. The stems dry and whither. Small black sclerotia, which look like rose thorns, appear in the rotting tissues. The sclerotia are the fruiting body (seed-pod type) of the fungus.

Control: Remove infested plants. The fungus lives in the soil, so do not plow under diseased plants. Practice crop rotation where possible.

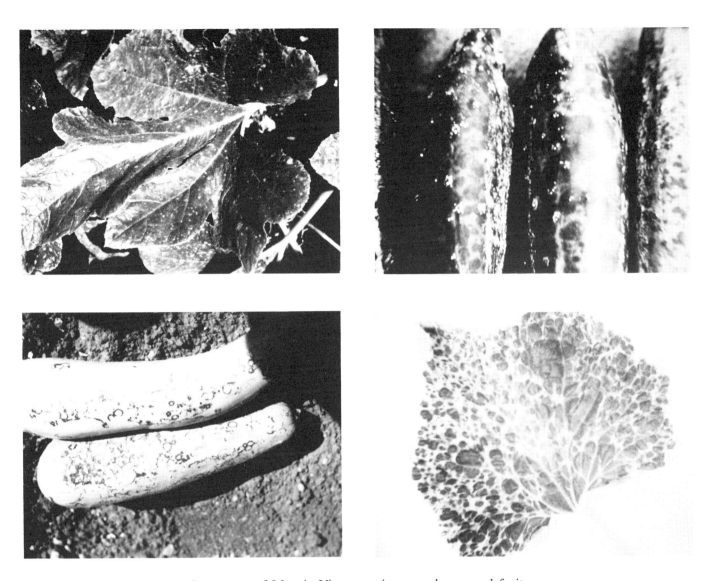

Symptoms of Mosaic Virus on vine crop leaves and fruit

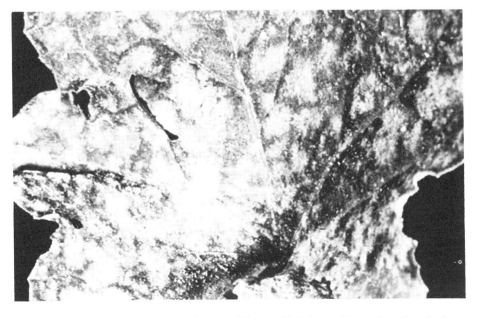

Powdery Mildew on Vine Crops. (Photo: U.S.D.A. Extension Service)

Bibliography and Additional Reading

American Horticultural Society. *Vegetables.* Franklin Center, PA: The Franklin Library, 1980.

Borror, Donald J., DeLong, Dwight M., and Triplehorn, Charles A. *Study of Insects.* Holt Rinehart and Winston, 1976.

Fell, Derek. *Vegetables, How to Select, Grow and Enjoy.* Tucson, AZ: HP Books, 1982.

Horts, R. Kenneth. *Westcott's Plant Disease Handbook.* New York: Van Nostrand Reinhold, 1979.

Little, V.A. *General and Applied Entomology.* Harper & Row Publishers, 1963.

MacNab, A.A., Sherf, A.F. and Springer, J.K. *Identifying Diseases of Vegetables.* University Park, PA: Pennsylvania State University College of Agriculture, 1983.

McCullagh, James C. *The Solar Greenhouse Book.* Emmaus, PA: Rodale Press, 1978.

Miller, Timothy. *Common Utah Vegetable Garden Pests.* Logan, UT: Utah State University Extension Service: Entomology Newsletter No. 71, 1984.

Organic Gardening magazine editors. *Getting the Most from Your Garden.* Emmaus, PA: Rodale Press, 1980.

Richardson, E. Arlo, and Hubbard, Kenneth, G. *Guide in Determining Multiple Plants Dates.* Logan, UT: Utah State University.

Thomson, Sherm. *Datatrieve Plant Disease File.* Logan, UT: Utah State University Extension Service, 1983.

University Of Idaho - Soil's Handbook. University of Idaho Extension Service, 1977.

Wescott, Cynthia. *The Gardener's Bug Book.* Garden City, NY: Doubleday & Company, 1973.

Wolf, Ray. *Solar Growing Frame.* Emmaus, PA: Rodale Press, 1980

Vegetable Seed Sources

Many of the better new varieties of vegetable seeds are not available in the packaged-seed trade outlets of the Intermountain West. These new hybrids are more expensive than what is found in the over-the-counter seed lines. They are available through many of the national mail order houses, which offer these new hybrids at competitive prices. The little extra cost will often pay off in sweeter crops, heavier yields and improved disease resistance.

Many of the national seed houses will send you a free catalog upon request. You will find excellent varieties, quality and prices in the following companies. There are also many other good suppliers.

Burpee Seed Company
300 Park Ave.
Warminster, PA 18974

Harris Seed Company
P.O. Box 22960
Rochester, NY 14692-2960

Park Seed Company
Greenwood, SC 29647

Stokes Seed Company
P.O. Box 548
Buffalo, NY 14240

Twilley Seed Company
P.O. Box 65
Trevose, PA 19053

Index

Index

Index